Cape Cod Therapy

Tom Simek

ISBN: 149472054X
ISBN-13: 978-1494720544

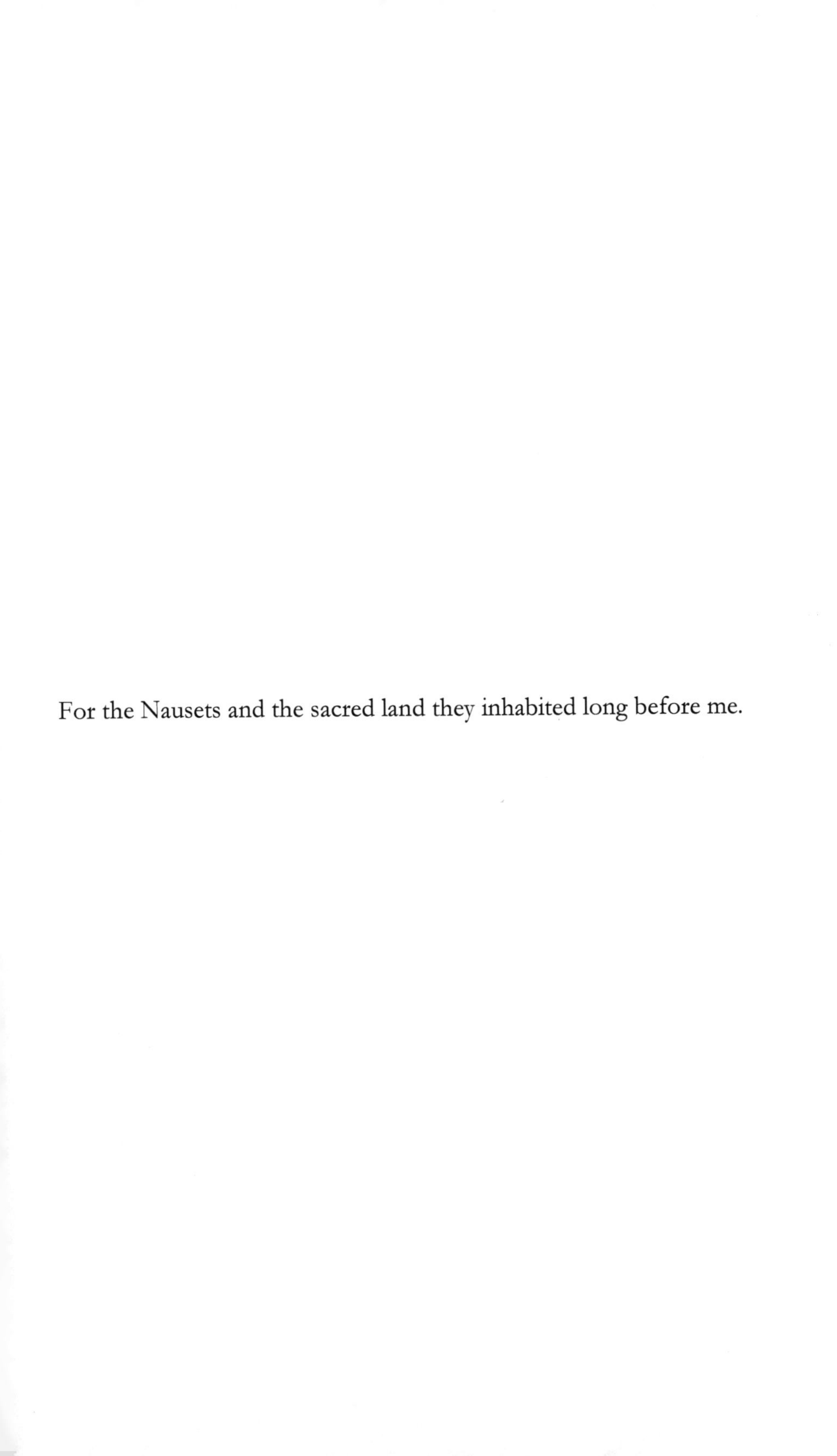

For the Nausets and the sacred land they inhabited long before me.

CONTENTS

ACKNOWLEDGMENTS

I would like to acknowledge my parents, Richard and Mary Ann Simek, their good friends Martha and Mike, and Susan and Ed, as well as the Cape Cod National Seashore and Briarwood Marine Science and Sailing Summer Camp.

Cover Photograph: Waves at Nauset Light Beach, North Eastham
Photography by Tom Simek. Design by Lara Melachrinou.

Photography:
Pages 7, 22, 29, 37, 56, 66, 75, 77, 86, 103 by Tom Simek.
Pages 4, 18, 37 by Lara Melachrinou.
Page 10 by Mary Ann Simek.
Pages 41, 61, 72, 79, 80 by Dan Simek.

1 INTRODUCTION

Cape Cod formed along the northeastern coast of the United States from the runoff of the North American ice sheet, a gigantic glacier, which deposited vast amounts of sand and sediment upon its retreat at the end of the last ice age. Like an afterthought finishing touch on the already inherently beautiful boundary between land and sea, Cape Cod literally is "the new world," as geologically speaking it's just a baby born a mere 18,000 years ago.

The results of its unusual birth are evident everywhere you look. You can see it in the oddly placed boulders scattered across the landscape, the vast stretches of uninterrupted sandy coastline and the numerous freshwater ponds which sit uneasily surrounded by a saltwater abyss. Cape Cod is the result of an unlikely contradiction, a delicate balance between fiercely opposing forces. It's a wonder the place even exists at all. One might suppose the furious North Atlantic would have devoured it long ago, but somehow that low-lying strip of land has found a fluxing balance with the hungry ocean.

The Cape's unique shape alone makes it magical. From the air, it's like a giant arm flexing its muscle eastward towards England, as if the land prematurely embodied the spirit of its later inhabitants, who would go on to defy monarchical Europe and reshape the modern political world forever. But in 1620, even before the American revolution, the new world gave a fresh start to religious pilgrims, who first landed on Cape Cod and decided to settle in its large, protected bay.

Like those pilgrims, Henry David Thoreau and so many others, I too found myself on Cape Cod and enchanted by its mystic allure. It's something you can only understand if you've experienced it, but once the Cape gets you, it never lets you go. I can say exactly when it got me.

I was seventeen and full of teenage angst, stuck in a small town and hanging out with all the wrong people. Landlocked and leashed, I longed for freedom maybe just a tiny bit like those pilgrims did nearly 400 years before.

One night in the darkest days of winter, my mind filled with dangerous thoughts. I'd had enough of high school and team sports, shallow girls and petty small town politics. It all felt like too much. I was sick of it and wanted out. So I got in my car and started driving.

I set off going nowhere in particular, just out of town, but the further I drove, the better I felt, so I kept on going. I had no intention of ending up where I did, but after five hours of driving late into the night, I ended up on Cape Cod. Maybe I went there simply because I knew the way, or maybe it was because that's where the highway ended. Either way, I like to think the spirit of the Cape drew me to her to protect me, because only there was I able to find refuge and cast away my demons.

I realized then for the first time that the ocean doesn't judge. It doesn't discriminate and ultimately it doesn't care. I needed some of that carefree mentality, to see and feel something bigger than myself. It was my first Cape Escape, my own pilgrimage for freedom and like the pilgrims, what I found was not what I had expected. She listened for a time, but then Mother Nature replied with blunt honesty. She could provide no sanctuary as there's no such thing as safety.

I arrived in the middle of the night, feeling liberated. But once I stopped at the water's edge, it all collapsed. Without a plan or even enough money to get back home, I stayed until sunrise, when the police found me. That surely wasn't the end of my problems, but it was the end of my insecurity. The Cape might not have shown me what I wanted to see, but it showed me exactly what I needed to. I am small, very small, but size isn't everything.

Like the Cape, we all live in a delicate balance on the edge of our imminent demise. Death is always a step away. It's a harsh reality to learn, but Cape Cod taught me it's better to face it than it is to spend your life running away from it. There's duality in everything and Mother Nature is two-faced as well. The only thing that matches her peaceful serenity is her savage viciousness. Summers on the Cape can be beautiful, but the winters are brutal and it's no place for the weak of heart.

The ocean is so much bigger than the Cape, but the Cape still survives not because it's solid and uncompromising, but interestingly enough because it's fluid like the water. The shores of Cape Cod can flex and bend without breaking. It moves, like the sea, is eaten in one place only to be spit out in another. It collapses here, is built up there and over time I've come to realize it's not so much a fight as it is a dance.

On Cape Cod, impermanence is undeniable. You can watch the world move before your eyes. The beaches are a shifting mass of sand that gets reshaped with each passing tide. A single storm can drastically modify the coastline and this continuous flux reveals that what we are seeing now is merely a snapshot in a feature length film, whose story will eventually end. Nothing lasts forever. Someday the sea will most likely win and Cape Cod will be gone. So will I. But that's ok. We're here now. The "here and now:" that's what the Cape really taught me.

It's easy to both get lost and lose yourself on Cape Cod. That's because it's like a zany, surreal world full of strange little quirks. What is called the "lower Cape" is actually geographically above the "upper Cape." So you can be traveling on "Route 6 North" and be heading due south. A sign might say you're driving east, but the compass will register west. You can watch the sunrise and sunset overlooking the water on the same day because Cape Cod has a coastline that faces in every direction, yet it is not an island. It's a cape.

Strong tides and shifting sandbars make Cape Cod a maze to navigate nautically, as some places have seven feet of water at high tide and are dry six hours later. Therefore, lighthouses were built all along the Cape's shores to serve as both sophisticated navigational markers and warning signs of danger ahead. Each lighthouse is equipped with a distinctive pattern of spinning lights, which from a distance looks like synchronized flashes. By using a catalogue of locations, captains (in the days before GPS) would plot their location by identifying the frequency of light flashes. The canal was then built to help ships altogether avoid the outer coast, which has been the graveyard to many sailors, including pirates.

According to Thoreau, Cape Cod's shores were so dangerous for ships that settlers had come to rely on the booty of shipwrecks, which washed up. There are even fantastic stories of cruel folks, who went so far as to fake the lighthouse signals in order to confuse the seafaring sailors and lure them, like sirens, to their demise. They were called "mooncussers" because only the light of the moon could supposedly foil their devious plans.

Much has changed since back then, but in some ways, the Cape, which Thoreau described a hundred and fifty years ago, is still very much the same. It's obviously a bit more developed, but thankfully much of its pristine outer coastline has remained preserved by the National Seashore, which was created in 1961 with the help of the Kennedy family (who are also enchanted Cape Codders).

Nauset Light, North Eastham.

The name Cape Cod was formed organically, being derived from its geological shape and the name of the fish, which were once found in abundance in its fertile waters. A hundred years ago, you could catch cod from shore, but over-fishing eventually devastated the local fish populations, so presently you have to travel far off shore to find such fish. In fact, the entire marine ecosystem of Cape Cod was nearly destroyed, but thankfully for some modern foresight and strict regulations, many of the once endangered species have returned and their populations are growing. The whales and seals have come back and with them have come the sharks as well.

The movie "Jaws" (1975) was filmed on Martha's Vineyard and has come to sensationalize our fears of these terrifying predators. But the truth is that sharks aren't bad. In fact, you might even call them good, as they're a necessary piece of the ecosystem.

After fishing regulations caused the local fish population to boom, the seals returned, which was good, at first. However, the seal population itself began to damage the fish population because of its own consumption rates, drawing the ire of fisherman, who had once been forced to sacrifice their yearly yield only to watch it get eaten up by the seals.

Many of the fishermen called for a good old-fashioned seal hunt, but it's no longer allowed since federal law protects the marine mammals. What to do? Cue the sharks, which have come back to naturally control the seal population. By reducing the number of seals, more large fish survive, which in turn eat the little fish and so on and so forth down the food chain, thereby creating a stable ecosystem.

Like everyone, I still have a natural fear of sharks, but Cape Cod has taught me to look beyond my fears and see how everything, even horrifying scary monsters like sharks, has a place in this world. Look at it from the shark's point of view. They're just hungry. Look at it from the seal's perspective. Well, they're just hungry as well and of course afraid of sharks.

Sometimes, after sitting on the beach all day, I start to wonder, does a seal know it's a seal? Does a shark know it's a shark? Does a seal ever wish it were a shark? Who knows? But seals seem pretty happy being seals, otherwise they wouldn't swim so fast to get away from the sharks. I know I'm not a seal or a shark. I'm a human, but I too will do what I must to survive. I too get hungry and scared and that means that I too must have a place somewhere in this mess. It took me quite some time to learn, but the Cape also taught me the most basic facts of life, that I too must fight hard to stay alive and be content with who and what I am.

2 SURFING

Cape Cod certainly isn't known as the surfing capital of the world. Although its pristine sandy beaches sometimes produce nice breaks, the weather and quality of waves is anything but consistent. Conditions can go from glassy, knee high rollers one day to blown-out double overhead sized waves the next. On top of that, the shifting sandbars and strong tides form swiftly flowing rip currents, which dramatically alter the waves' break throughout the day.

The water on Cape Cod is generally cold. On the outer beaches the average temperature only reaches a still-chilly high in the upper 60's in August and a bone chilling low in the mid to upper 30's in early March. So, for much of the year, it's a struggle just to brave the frigid water. Wet suits are needed, even in the summer, especially on big wave days when the churning sea doesn't allow the sun to heat the surface. Thick wet suits and even dry suits (with a hood and booties) are a must in the spring, late fall and winter months.

As much of a pain as wetsuits are to get on and off, like all things I've learned to love them for a number of reasons. First, wet suits are cool. Put one on and you feel like a superhero. Whether or not you look like one is a different story, but who cares how you look? Surfers don't. Secondly, wetsuits protect your skin so you can stay out on the water all day without having to worry about sunburn or board rash (from the wax on the board chaffing your skin).

After I got my first wetsuit at age 8, I went out with a boogie board, got one good ride and that's all it took. I was hooked. I worked the waves like a summer job, everyday from 11-7 and little by little I gained valuable field experience, developed a feel for the board and got acquainted with the forces of buoyancy and surface tension. I studied the ocean and learned about waves, which I've come to see as almost living things.

Waves at Nauset Light Beach, North Eastham.

A wave is simply a pulse of energy moving through the water and in order to ride that wave you must be able to tap into its energy by anticipating it. When a wave breaks, its energy gets released and during those brief moments when it's breaking incredible things happen. Water defies gravity. It rises up and sucks up more water around it, until the wave reaches a point when its mass outweighs its energy and gravity rips it back down.

Theoretically, surfing is about mastering physics and hydrodynamics, two things most people don't often associate with surfers. But here's the breakdown. The buoyancy of the board makes the rider less heavy in the water and the friction on the flowing water serves to further counteract gravity. A surfer uses the rise of the wave to push them across the surface of the water.

The fin or fins on the bottom of the board give the rider control by steering the flow of water underneath the board. Therefore, the smaller the waves you have, the bigger the board you'll need because you get less energy and only a small amount of acceleration. To counteract this, a bigger board provides more buoyancy for a rider going slow. On big waves, which contain more energy, you need just the opposite. Since there is a large drop and more energy, you can rely on forward momentum to keep you from breaking the surface tension of the water and stay afloat. Moreover, short boards allow short, quick turns, maneuverability, which is helpful in big waves.

The board is your tool and when you're surfing, it's your best friend because it allows you to do what ordinarily wouldn't be able to be done. Therefore, having the right board is key. If you have too small of a board on a small wave day, you won't be able to ride, because you'll sink into the water. On the other hand, if you have too big of a board on a big day, you'll get your butt kicked fighting with the long board and trying to control it in the faster break.

A breaking wave depends predominantly on a trio of factors: amplitude, frequency and water depth. Amplitude is how high the waves are, frequency is the distance between the waves and depth is obviously how deep the water is. The atmosphere supplies the energy for the force, but geography shapes where and how the waves break. Because of these varying factors, some waves break fast and some waves break slow. Some waves break parallel to the beach, others at an angle. But all waves are endowed with the same inner force and like people no two waves are the same or have lives that break in exactly the same way.

A "good break" occurs when these factors combine favorably to create balanced waves. These waves don't break haphazardly. They seem to hang there and roll in at a steady and constant rate. Good breaks first require good waves, which usually start as deep-ocean swells kicked up from storms offshore. Once you have that key ingredient, a good break can be created in a number of ways, but generally there are two types of breaks: breaks on points and breaks in bays.

Point breaks occur when waves break on an emerged or submerged peninsula sticking out off of the coast. These waves start to break at one point, which results in two breaks moving out in opposite directions. A bay break occurs when a wave breaks while going into a bay. These two wave-breaks start at opposite ends and break inward toward each other, eventually "closing out" at some point in the middle. (Note: A "close out" is when a wave completes its break, leaving the rider with no more wave face to ride.)

So if you want to go surfing, you can't just go anyplace. You can only surf (on Cape Cod in particular) at the right place at the right time and it's not just about the waves and the geography. It's also about the wind, which needs to be blowing in the right direction and the tide, which needs to be at the right place in its cycle. Therefore surfers, like all people, are at the mercy of their environment. No matter what you might believe. You are not in control. When you're in the ocean, the ocean is boss.

Surfing is not about being fearless. To be fearless is foolish. Fear is good. It's a natural warning sign of danger,.and while surfing you are always in danger because the act of surfing is dangerous. So is life. Surfing, like living, requires you to simultaneously conquer your natural fears while continuing to recognize potential hazards. Surfers love the ocean. It's a god to them and as any gentile knows a god must be respected and feared. Like most land lovers, it took me a while to really fear the sea.

The first time I ate it was when I was really little. I was playing at the edge of the beach where the water was washing up from a shore break (when the waves are breaking directly onto the sand). I was in the impact zone (where the waves break) and got sucked up in the backwash. The next wave lifted me up, flipped me over and slammed me back down on my back. After that, I was a little more careful where I played.

The next time I really got disciplined was when I was ten. I got caught in an undertow (a current of water under the surface) and was dragged along with my board out beyond the breakers. My mom and a lifeguard, who had been watching me, signaled for me to come back in closer.

I paddled out of the current, just like I had learned to do, but as I was paddling back toward the beach, a set of waves came and I inadvertently rode the biggest wave I had ever ridden up to that point in my life. I got a great ride, but it only lasted a hot second before I bit it hard and was put through the washing machine.

I tumbled and turned around through the churning whitewater. The wave washed me all the way into shore and spit me out on the beach. After that I was a bit more careful with what waves I chose to ride.

Surfing at Nauset Light Beach, North Eastham.

I learned to fear my board after I got hit in the back of the head with it and I learned to fear other surfers when someone ran into me. Then, as I grew, I got enlightened yet again when I tried to paddle out during a summer storm. The waves were gigantic, but blown out, so they were breaking with no sense of order. It was just chaotic oceanic rage.

I fought for an hour to break through the walls of advancing water, paddling and ducking, paddling and ducking, trying to push my way through the waves. But after all of the fighting I turned around to see that I was still only about ten yards offshore and had been pushed about a mile down the beach.

The ocean is a force that can't be reckoned with. It's merciless and cruel, with no care or caution. It'll eat you up and spit you out. It's unforgiving. There's no room for mistake, no compromising and no stopping it.

Every time you enter the ocean, whether you are surfing or wading, you're at its mercy. Respect it. Don't ever turn your back on the ocean. It's like war. Know yourself and your enemy. However, the ocean is a foe you cannot conquer. You can only fight it or, like surfers, you can learn to temporarily align yourself with it.

It's hard to describe the sheer ecstasy of riding a wave. It's Zen. Your mind completely blanks out. You stop thinking and acknowledge the totality of existence. For surfers, it's not "I think, therefore I am," it's "I surf, therefore I am." Because when you're riding a wave, you're there. You're exactly where you are. You're not thinking about the past or the future. You're not even thinking, you're just doing.

When on a wave, it's like nothing else in the world exists and for that brief period of time, nothing else matters. You're completely centered and in perfect harmony with the world around you, so surfing is spiritual and highly addictive because it's thrilling. Once you get one good ride, you just want to get another…and another.

Since the conditions on Cape Cod are most times less than ideal, surfing there often involves a lot of waiting. Thus I learned both patience and the importance of taking advantage of opportunity as it arises. When it's happening it's happening. The waves are there and everything is great. But when it's not happening and the waves aren't there there's nothing a surfer can do but hope and pray. I can't count the number of hours I've spent lazily bobbing up and down on my board looking out at the horizon, silently begging for a little action to come my way. I've gone out for both tide changes to get only a single ride. But that one ride makes it worth your while.

It happens like this: You're bobbing up and down on the waves and first you see the swell coming in from far out. It starts as a bulge on the horizon and as it moves in you start to get an idea of its size and calculate how far out it's likely to break. Then you set out to position yourself at the right place in time so that you can catch the wave just as it starts to crest. If you're too far out, the swiftly moving swell will pass right underneath you and you'll miss it. If you're too far in, it'll break on top of you.

Like a magical, mystical world, the entrance to a wave is only open for a split second, so timing is everything. You have to prepare yourself by building up some speed and paddling in toward shore, then propel yourself down the front of the wave just as it's cresting. Once you feel the force propelling you, you must quickly pop up and distribute your weight evenly over the rising water to counteract gravity.

In many ways, just initially getting up onto the board is more difficult than staying up, because you have to go from your chest to your feet in a second. From there, you enter a majestic state of being, in which you feel almost like your floating or levitating. It's hard to describe. You're not completely weightless, but it feels a bit like suspended animation. Time seems to slow. Your sense of self disappears.

When riding a wave, your actions must be fluid and smooth, like the wave because every tiny movement comes with big consequences. You can easily wipe out hard just by shifting your weight slightly. It's like learning to ride a bike. You have to practice. It's awkward and clumsy at first. The balance is so difficult to find and so easy to lose.

It's one thing to understand surfing and another to actually do it. A scientist may be able to explain the mechanics, but that doesn't mean they can put it into practice. That's something you have to find out for yourself. The ocean is always there. The waves are always breaking. You can go out day after day and even if that magical world might sit right before your eyes, you may never find it, but trust me it's there.

Surfing is more than just physics. It's a metaphysical art and a religious practice. The energy in those waves came from the basic energy that fuels everything in our universe. So when you're riding a wave, you're not just riding the disturbances in our atmosphere. You're riding the ancient cosmic energy, which is leftover from creation, the big bang, and still reverberates today.

When you meld yourself with that energy and become a part of that flow, the "you" you think exists ceases to be and you see that you're just a tiny piece of something larger. Call it God, call it Allah, call it Nirvana, call it whatever you like. It's the feeling that counts, not the words. Some people access it by praying at a holy sight. To me, the act of surfing is sacred and the ocean is my temple.

3 SAILING

Sailing was the original "green" transportation, because it relies solely on renewable resources and doesn't require any fossil fuels. You just need a little bit of turbulence in the atmosphere and a means to harness that energy. Whereas while surfing you ride the wave, the energy created by the wind, when sailing you ride the wind itself.

Sailing was at the forefront of transportation and trade for thousands of years, until the steam engine rendered it obsolete. So why isn't this mode of transport more prevalent today? The answer is simple: speed and reliability. Sailing doesn't fit well into our highly scheduled and organized economic system, because it is sometimes slow going and often unreliable. These attributes might not be good for business or the bottom line, but to me they're what make sailing so fun.

You can't sail without wind, so while sailing you are, as always, completely at the mercy of the natural world and its elements. When there's no wind, all you do is drift. I can only imagine how much of a nuisance this must have been to early traders and explorers, who found themselves stuck in the middle of the ocean for days and sometimes weeks with sagging sails.

Also akin to surfing, sailing is all about basic physics, but uses vectors (directional force) to create mobility. The two basic forces at work in sailing are opposing: wind and resistance (drag). Everything starts from the wind. The wind provides the power for the sails to catch. You have no control over the power of the wind. You only have control over how much resistance you give to it by positioning the boat and the sails accordingly.

A sailboat is propelled by the redirection of force. The wind, which is harnessed in the sails, serves not to push the boat, but rather to pull it. The force from the wind is transferred to the mast (the pole the sails are raised on), which is attached to the hull (the actual boat) and provides the energy to propel the vessel.

The direction and speed of a sailboat's movement are derived from two angles, the angle of the wind going into the sails and the angle of the keel underneath the boat. By properly controlling these two variables it becomes possible to travel anywhere you want, even somewhat magically upwind. The truth is that you can't travel directly into the wind, but you can travel diagonally towards it. You can always get where you want to go, you might just have to go someplace else first. In order to do this, you must tack.

Tacking is the maneuver of turning into the wind and a series of tacks forms a zig-zag pattern going opposite its flow. When tacking upwind, you can't just go straight to your destination. You have to strategically direct yourself there by going different places first, taking preparatory steps to your goal. The boat may never actually point at the place you have your sights set on until you arrive. So even if you know where you want to go, you never know exactly how you're going to get there. It all depends on where the wind and the tides will take you and I've learned that if you let it, the wind will take you to some pretty unexpected and amazing places.

While in theory sailing is rather basic, the practice of it is not. Sailing takes much more than just logic to understand. It demands acute observation and intuition. For example, one might logically deduce that you'll travel fastest when traveling directly with the wind. But this isn't true. You actually go faster at an angle somewhat perpendicular to the wind, at a point where the forces maximize their potential. Going into the wind obviously doesn't give you any power in your sails, but going directly with the wind increases the drag of your boat, which must plow through the water, whereas going sideways and slightly downwind (a run) makes for the fastest way to travel because you have the optimal combination of a lot of force and little drag.

Therefore, while sailing, you are constantly forced to adjust and alter your course based on these two factors and you quickly find out that the quickest way is not always the shortest. It's like taking a less direct highway instead of a more direct country road. But to me, the real beauty of sailing is not about going fast or getting someplace in a hurry. In our fast paced world, sailing is a nice excuse to chill out and go slow. What's the rush anyway? We're constantly running from place to place, spending much of our time and energy in transit. I'm here, but I want to be there. I have this, but I want that. Sailing is living in and enjoying the time in between. It's important to know where you're going, but it's even more important to understand where you are and sailing definitely makes you aware of that.

Like Buddhism, sailing teaches mindfulness and awareness. It has taught me to pay attention to the little things, which I normally take for granted, most obviously the wind. Most people in everyday life only notice the wind when it becomes strong enough to become an inconvenience for them or maybe offers them some relief from heat. When you're sailing, the wind becomes your local compass. Whether it's strong or weak, you pay attention to every little gust that blows your way.

The tricky part is that you can't actually see the wind. You can only feel and observe its effects. It's like a phantom, which leaves you clues to decipher. You can feel it on your lips. It blows through the trees and ripples across the surface of the water. You can see it in the clouds and the way birds fly. But when sailing the wind is only half of the battle. The other half is a world, which you must be equally aware of and also goes unseen. It's the world that lies hidden underneath the water.

A sailboat draws quite a lot of water (because of the keel or center board that sticks down below it), so knowing the depth of the water is absolutely essential. Around Cape Cod, most underwater hazards are marked, but there are still many places where rocks and sandbars are hidden. You can't see much of what's under the water, but you can hypothesize by watching what's above it. The geography of the land around can provide some clues about how the underwater landscape might be. You can also watch currents and the ways the waves are breaking, both of which give insight into how deep the water is. But, as in life, there are always random, unexpected hazards.

Another grave concern to sailors are currents and tides, which can not only aid or inhibit progress, but also vary the depth of the water throughout the day. As I mentioned in the introduction, Cape Cod is notoriously tricky to navigate even in charted waters (that's why they built the canal and have buoyed harbors and shipping lanes). Sailing forces you to develop foresight. You can't just analyze the environment as it is, you have to be able to anticipate how it is going to be in the near future and plan accordingly. You don't want to go out in a light wind and end up getting stuck out there if the wind dies. You also don't want to go out at high tide and get stuck coming back in at low tide. Not surprisingly, for sailors, like surfers, the weather becomes an obsession.

Wind is essentially just the movement of air from high pressure to low pressure systems caused by the uneven heating of the Earth's surface. Being able to read the clouds and changes in barometric pressure can make all the difference in preventing you from getting stuck out in a squall. Floating on the water with a forty-foot metal pole sticking up above you is not the best place to be in a thunderstorm, and once you find yourself in a situation like that, it's already too late. Therefore, prevention is key.

You have to learn not to simply react, as most people often do, but to act in anticipation. In high winds, you have to be ready at all times to let the sails out and in low winds you have to be ready to catch every small gust. When the weather's perfect and the wind is right, it's smooth sailing, but inclement weather is what really puts your skills on trial. As in life, stressful situations test your metal. You have to be able to come through in high-pressure situations and make the right move when there is little room for error or you can easily find yourself ship-wrecked. Logic doesn't always help when you're in a make or break situation. Sometimes, you only have a single chance to make the right decision and any hesitation will cause you to miss the opportunity. Therefore, decisions must be swift and decisive.

In sailing, as in life, it's quite easy to find yourself floundering around. So if you want to get anywhere, you have to plot your course, commit to it and take control of whatever variables you can. When you make a mistake learn what went wrong. Minor mistakes early on can help you avoid disaster later. That's how you build experience, your most trusted ally. Maybe some people are more inclined to be sailors than others, but sailors are not born. Old salts are made over time because there's so much more to sailing (and living) than working the equipment properly.

Every day is different and even if you've seen a thousand similar ones, you never know what a day is going to bring. You can never have enough experience because there will always be situations, which you cannot foresee or predict. Therefore, you have to learn to improvise.

Every new experience gives you a better ability to deal with the unique challenges you will inevitably face. Maybe you have never faced exactly those conditions before, but you might have faced something similar. Some solutions have the ability of solving multiple problems. Duct tape works for most everything and applying your previous knowledge can help make difficult situations easy to overcome. The more tools you have in your mental toolbox, the greater your ability is to solve problems.

Boats, in general, are notoriously finicky. The salt water wreaks havoc on the integrity of a vessel and the boat, being a bit like a body, begins to break down from the moment it's been fully built. The metal rusts, the glue un-sticks, the seals fail, the wood warps and the sheets tear. The natural tendency of chaos takes over. What was once tight becomes loose. Pieces break and water slowly seeps its way in.

I was once tacking in a strong wind and had a side-stay (one of the tension cables used to keep the mast straight) rip the threads right out of the nut. I was greatly frightened when it popped and saw the mast undulating back and forth above me. After that, I was a bit more careful with my tacks and jibes, so beyond the natural elements you have to also be conscious of your equipment and wary of its limits as well.

A tricky aspect of boating in general is that boats don't have brakes. In order to stop yourself or slow down your forward momentum, you can only apply force in the opposite direction. The closest thing you have to an e-brake while sailing is going into what's known as "irons."

Whenever the wind is too strong and the boat starts to heel (tilt to the side) too much, you have two options to remedy the situation. You can either put out the sails a little or point the boat more into the direction of the wind, thus dumping some of the wind from the sails.

"Irons" is the result of doing both simultaneously. It's a state of being really, when you offer the least amount of resistance. You steer the ship directly into the wind and let out all of the lines. The sails start flapping and the boat essentially stalls, by seizing forward momentum.

"Irons" will slow you down, but in won't by any means stop you from drifting in the current or the wind. It's easy to get to on a standard single-mast (two-sailed) boat, like the ones most people sail for recreational purposes, but I can only imagine what it must have been like to sail one of those big wooden multi-masted beasts they sailed back in the golden age of sailing.

Those captains must have been more skilled than an airline pilot to handle those ships and all of their complexities because those ships often had dozens of sails, which were all connected to the boat by numerous lines. There were no computer navigational systems, no engines and no weather forecasts. Plus, they were working without highly synthesized materials, like wood and plant fibers, which easily fray and break. Therefore, boat maintenance then and today is still a top priority.

Some of those poor souls went through hell on the high seas: broken masts, hidden shoals and windless days. The hazards are innumerable and I can just picture all of the sailors trapped in the middle of the ocean for weeks, dehydrated and surrounded by an abyss of water they couldn't drink. And what about the unfortunate ones who were traveling in late summer and found themselves in the path of a hurricane? Then again, I wonder if those old seadogs had any fear.

Those pioneers seemed to be as bold and brave as they come, often departing places uncertain if they would ever return. Those early explorers were chasing something, which I think goes to the core of humanity. Humans naturally wonder, as much as we fear. Sailors simply choose to live their lives following the wonder, not the fear. Imagine if you could live unafraid, unafraid of death, unafraid to fail, unafraid of risks and unafraid of what other people might think, imagine what you might accomplish.

Tall ship in Provincetown harbor.

Sailors know that fear is limiting. But don't be mistaken, living without fear doesn't mean not taking precautions and not being careful. Again, that's just plain stupidity. You can't be blamed for not doing something you can't do, but you can be blamed for not trying to do something you could. Therefore, act boldly and with intent, and like the boy scouts say "always be prepared." Because once you get out there in the wind and the waves, it's already too late. Be ready for each and every voyage you take, whether it's large or small.

Many people have left dry land for the seas never to return. Some were lost in the deep and dark abyss, but others just so happened to chance upon pristine shores in wonderful places, like Cape Cod, and chose to never go back. That's the true spirit of sailing. It matters where you're going, not how fast.

4 FISHING

I can sit for hours waiting for the pole to move. Some people say it's boring, but to me fishing is another excuse to slow down in this fast paced world and it's extremely exciting when you do actually catch something. Fishing teases you. It makes you wait and wait, but that wait only makes the catch more thrilling.

Fishing so perfectly taps into our predatory instincts to chase and capture. The hunt. It feels good. Jesus was a fisherman and to me it's another type of meditation. You can go in a group, but most of the time is spent in silence, like monks in a temple. It's better that way. It gives you time to think, to focus and concentrate on your thoughts.

Maybe it's more like prayer, when you're full of hope that something good is going to happen, to catch that big one. But if not, that's ok too. At least you were at the ocean all day and that can be in itself enough to make fishing worthwhile.

Just sitting there, you start to notice things you wouldn't normally look at and you start thinking things you wouldn't normally think about. Sometimes I start to wonder what it was like fishing back in the day before synthetic lines and swiveling reels. What if I only had my bare hands and whatever else I could find? I'd never be able to catch a fish that way. But what if I was going to starve? Then maybe I would. I'd figure out a way…or would I even bother? Maybe I'd go for something that's easier to get.

Catching fish, like so many other things, is all about timing and placement. The fish aren't going to come to you. You've got to go to them at the right time of day when the tide is right with the right equipment. For being such a seemingly passive activity, fishing takes a whole lot of work just to access and set up properly to get the fish from the sea onto the shore (or into the boat.)

When a fish hits, there's a burst of excitement. The top of the poll drops and if it's a big one the line starts going out. The first order of business when you get a fish "on" is making sure the hook is set or you might lose it. There are various techniques to accomplish this, but the most basic is a light, but firm tug on the line, while keeping tension on it at all times.

The next and equally important step is setting the drag. The drag is the resistance you give to the line. You must immediately and accurately adjust the drag based on the size of the fish or how much the fish is fighting. Note that this must be done without actually being able to see how big the fish is.

As with most activities, setting the drag is about balance because it's give and get. If you set the drag tight, you take more line in quicker and the reel becomes harder to turn. With the drag set tightly you run the risk of breaking the line if the fish is big. So you have to give yourself some room for error. If you loosen the drag, the reel becomes easier to turn because you're taking in less line. This makes for a longer fight and more of a chance that the hook will come out. The most effective way to fish is to incrementally tighten the drag as the fish tires out and gets closer in when there's less line and more control. But you always want to make sure to give a little if needed as to not break the line. Once the fish is gone it's gone. It's better to take your time and get the fish than be hasty and lose it.

Fishing makes for a strange fight, because in some ways it's so impersonal. First of all, fish are fish. It's not like hunting another mammal, when you feel like you have a whole lot in common with it. Fish are cold blooded and live under water, so it's harder to associate one's self with it. Plus, you can't even see it when you're fighting it, unless the fish happens to come to the surface. If you're surfcasting, your vision is often blocked by waves and you'll probably never see the fish until you get it onto shore. All you can do is feel it.

The pole, which yes sounds a bit phallic, is like both a weapon and a trap. The initial objective of fishing is to deceive the fish into taking the bait, while the final objective always remains to get the fish out of the water. Fish yield substantial power and ability in their native environment, but once outside it, in the air and on dry land, a fish's abilities are starkly limited.

Some fish are very particular with what they bite, so baiting a hook can be an art in itself. It's tricky enough when you're using frozen or fresh bait, but even trickier when using live bait. You have to make sure to secure the bait, but also to hide or disguise the hook in order to maintain the bait's integrity.

Surf Casting at Nauset Light Beach, North Eastham.

Using a lure can be just as touchy in its own right because you have to use your pole like a puppet string and put life into the mock fish. To catch a fish, you have to think like a fish. You must "be the fish."

Certain lures, when wielded by a skilled hand look lifelike in the water and those are the ones that usually catch the big ones. Spinners are probably the easiest lure to use because you can just reel in at a constant rate and some fish, if they're hungry, will bite just about anything that's moving.

So your method of fishing depends solely on your opponent. In fishing, like in life, you should do whatever works. If you're catching fish, keep doing what you're doing. If you're not, then you've got to change things up, what you're using, where you're going or both. Either way, fishermen don't give up because fishing is addictive.

Like surfing a wave, once you catch one, you'll want to catch another. But you mustn't get greedy and take too much. I was taught this lesson the hard way on Cape Cod.

One afternoon in early July when I was a teen I was surfcasting with my father and older brother on the south side of Nauset Light Beach. Our prospects were looking good because earlier in the day, I had seen a flock of birds accompanying a school of blues not far off shore.

So the three of us camped out with a bucket, a cooler and a tackle box. The tide was high so the waist high rollers were breaking close in and we could easily cast our lines out beyond their break. We baited our lines with some fresh (not live) sand eels (a small bait fish), cracked open some beers and sat in the sand with our three fishing rods spread out some twenty or so yards from each other.

Nothing much happened until my brother spotted a flurry of swirling birds dropping down into the water offshore and down the beach some distance. We took one of our poles out of the water and put a lure on it just so we could be ready to cast and recast into the school if it happened to come in close enough.

The wandering school slowly migrated along the coast and drifted in closer to the beach. We took another line out of the water and tied a lure to it, preparing for our attack. But the school passed by us still too far out for us to reach. So my brother and I followed the group of fish up the beach and at one point it came in close enough to see the frenzy of splashing but remained still too far away for our casts. Then the school shifted course and wandered into deeper water, so my brother and I returned to my father, disappointed.

But we didn't stop watching the meandering school being chased by birds. When the school was almost out of sight, my brother noted how it had come in closer, but by that point it was at least a half a mile up the beach.

Without consciously thinking, my hunter instincts kicked in and I sprung into action. I grabbed another lure from the tackle box, just in case and took off running up the beach after the fish. I ran and ran and ran on the fringe of the beach where the whitewater washes up, stops and recedes back, being the hardest part of the sand and the easiest place to run. I followed the path the waves made for me and was huffing and puffing as I watched the school continue to move farther away up the coast. I didn't look back. I just kept on going and finally caught up to the moving mass, which I trailed parallel to along the beach.

Without warning, the school suddenly and swiftly switched direction and rushed in toward the shore. I didn't even have enough time to get my pole together before it was just beyond the breakers. My first cast sailed straight into the madness.

A fish hit immediately and I don't know if it was because the fish was big or if I had the drag set too tight but the line snapped as soon as I gave it my first tug and I yelled in frustration at my fluttering line, which I quickly reeled in. Experience had given me the foresight to bring another lure, just in case, so I tied it on.

While sitting there with the line in my hand, I watched the school descend upon the shore in a maelstrom of fury. The big blue fish were chasing the smaller baitfish onto shore and were lunging out of the waves to feast. Fish were literally swimming up onto the beach and getting swept back with the turbulence of the retreating waves. I realized then, in the worst of moments, that I didn't know how to tie a good fishing knot since my father and brother had always tied them for me.

Without thinking, I hastily tied a double half-square knot, being the knot my hands just so happened to muster up at that moment. I stood up, loosened the drag and threw my line out into the chaotic splashing and nothing!

I tried again and immediately, bam! A fish hit. It was so close to shore that I didn't even have to reel. I just firmly kept tension on the line and walked backwards up the beach, dragging the fish out of the water and onto the sand. The school of fish was still right there in front of me and I wanted to get another one.

There are two main types of game fish on the shores of Cape Cod. They are bluefish (blues) and striped bass (stripers). Stripers are named for the stripes they have running down their sides. They offer a mild, white meat, tend to be more solitary and have absolutely no teeth. Blues, on the other hand, are named for their blue-ish tint, tend to travel in schools and have very sharp teeth. It's obvious which kind of fish I was dealing with.

My father had told me those facts my whole life and I too knew exactly what kind of fish it was because I was looking at it. But in that moment, I didn't think. In my limited foresight, I had brought an extra lure, but hadn't taken along one of the most important tools a fisherman can have: a pair of pliers. Greedy eyes blinded me. I reached my fingers into the fish's mouth to pull out the hook so I could cast it out and bag another.

The moment I touched the lure, I saw the teeth and went to pull my fingers out, but before I could, the fish, with its gills fighting in the air, took one bite down with its mouth. It was like one last rebuke from that fish before it died, a big "F.U." revenge against me, its killer. I swear that fish looked me straight in the eye as it chomped down on my finger.

The teeth passed through my skin like a warm knife through butter and the blood started running out of the slices right away. I grabbed my finger and screamed in pain, cursing the fish and myself for my stupidity. I stomped around the beach yelling at the fish, which was still attached to the end of the line and slowly suffocating to death. He got me and I have to admit, if I were in the fish's position, I probably would have done the same thing. I didn't need another fish. The one I had caught was plenty big enough to feed my family. I should have known better. Take only what you need and no more. That's the lesson the Cape taught me that day.

Afterwards, I had to lug the fish's body back down the beach about a mile and a half, bleeding the whole way. I couldn't play the guitar for two weeks after and as a musician it was torture. Call it what goes around comes around or karma or whatever. I'll admit the fish got me good all right, but I got the last laugh when I ate him that night.

Some people say they can't kill something because they feel bad for it. The truth is you should feel bad for whatever meat you eat because that animal died so that you could live. I think people are better off killing their own meals, even if it is sometimes difficult and unsettling. When you kill something, you are aware of its death and in a way that simple awareness and acknowledgement pays honor and tribute to your prey. You must respect the fish as its predator and it's much easier to respect something when you knew it as it lived.

I had fought that fish. I had seen it swimming and although it was a worthy opponent, I had bested it and thus earned the right to eat it. There is a direct connection, an intimate relationship between the fish and me. It even tasted my blood before it died. Death is cruel, but it's nature's ritual self-sacrifice. To ignore it is to ignore the natural order of things. You can choose to be ignorant of it, but ignorance doesn't change the facts.

That night, I took the fish's remains and threw them back into the ocean for the crabs and other scavengers to feast on. There's no need for the remains of the fish to fester in a plastic bag in a landfill, where its carcass won't go to good use. It was my peace offering on the alter of the sea, giving back a piece of what it had given me. Plus, the speedy disposal of a filleted fish is absolutely necessary and the quicker the better. One time I left the remains of a fish in the garbage outside for a couple of days during the summer and it smelled so bad I couldn't even approach it without dry heaving.

Fishing sure is a dirty business, but so is life. It's messy and smelly and sometimes you've got to get your hands dirty to get the job done. Fishy smelling fingers are a part of it. You can wash your hands as many times as you'd like but that poignant aroma doesn't wash away so easily. It's part of the package and you've got to live with the guts and the grime if you want fresh fish.

Sure, you can buy fresh fish at the supermarket, fish store or fancy restaurant, but it's just not the same as watching the fish become food and being a part of that process. You might earn the money to buy the fish, but that feeling of accomplishment just isn't the same. If I had to choose between working to make the money to buy the fish or simply going out fishing to get the fish, I'd spend my time going directly after the fish.

Of course, I don't think I have the gall to actually be a commercial fisherman for many reasons, but doing anything for money fundamentally changes the nature of the act. Intent is important, like with killing the fish. My intent wasn't malicious. I killed the fish to fulfill a basic need. To kill without purpose is wrong. Wrong is going against the natural order. Getting eaten by a shark would be a terrible fate, but at least if it ate you, your death would serve a purpose. You can't blame the shark. It's just hungry. Terrifying, as it would be, wouldn't that be better than dying in some senselessly mundane way, like a vending machine accident?

Death is death, either way you're dead in the end. That fish died, but it lives on in me and not just in my memory. Its physical material literally became a part of me, so in a way, I owe a piece of everything I've done since that day to the fish and the sacrifice it unwillingly made for me.

5 CLAMMING

Clamming is essentially just digging in the sand, which can be fun in itself. But the part which some people don't really like is being knee deep in gooey, sticky and oftentimes smelly muck. The odor is partially created by the release of methane from microorganisms and methane is the same gas contained in flatulence, so you get the drift about how it smells.

On the contrary, that smell is a good thing because it means the soil is fertile and filled with life-nourishing nutrients, which probably are harboring clams and other critters. Coincidentally, the mud is also very good for the skin and some people pay big money for that type of skin treatment in spas. Out on the sand flats you can bathe in it for free if you want and the truth is, it will leave your skin feeling silky smooth. I know because I've done it, not because I wanted to or necessarily enjoyed it, but because the mud is also quite useful for keeping off the carnivorous flies.

Green-headed horse flies hurt when they bite and tiny no-see-ums can be maddening, especially in the earlier and later hours of the day when the wind is calm and the insects come out to go about their business. Therefore, it's most fun to go clamming in the middle of the day when there's a little bit of a breeze because if the bugs are out, they will easily drive you insane.

The best part of clamming and what makes it worthwhile, despite the nuisances, is the act of discovery. Whereas fishing appeals to our hunting instincts, clamming appeals to our gathering ones. It's foraging for food and feels a bit like a treasure hunt. (And currently it kind of is at the price clams are being sold at.) But clamming is not so much a trophy sport, like fishing, when you're often trying to bag the biggest fish you can. Clams are generally more tender when they're young. It's not good to eat them when they're too small for population reasons. The big ones tend to be tougher (good for stews). But the sweetness of clams and of life is found in the middle, between the two extremes.

To be successful in finding clams, like finding fish, you have to know where to go and when to go. You can't find something that's not there and even if you know it's there, you have to find a means to get it. The easiest place to access clams by hand is on tidal flats, in places where the sand holds a specific density and never completely dries out at low tide. There, you can use a clamming fork to search the sand. But my preferred method of clamming for quahogs is with bare feet, getting down and dirty, trudging through the trenches, using no tools other than your own anatomy. The clams hide. You seek.

You can just slowly walk around tidal pools, feeling around with the soles of your feet and trying to detect something that feels like a rock buried beneath the sand. Note that there are some hazards, like sharp broken shells and crabs, which will occasionally pinch your feet. But those tiny hazards give it a twist and touch of danger. Like any good game, there are risks and rewards.

Steamers (soft shelled clams) are a bit trickier to catch, because they're phenomenal diggers. You can dig them with your hands, but your fingers will get cut up from the sharp edges of their shells. They're quick little buggers, so you have to sneak up on them and take them by surprise. Once you let them start moving in the sand, they've got a good chance of getting away.

Digging arbitrarily is just a waste of energy. You should scan the surface of the sand for places where you can see a little hole. Sometimes there's a bump or even an indentation, which gives away the clam's location. If you're good, you can quickly put your fork in the sand and scoop them up before they dig deeper.

Just like when fishing, while shell fishing it helps to watch the birds. They'll tip you off to areas where life is rich and abundant. Coastal birds are clever when it comes to finding their meals. We might call dumb people "bird brains," but birds are smarter than we think and I've witnessed their intelligence.

Since the clams' shells are too hard for the birds to break with their beaks, the birds use an innovative solution to accomplish their work. They grab the clam and then fly high above hard ground (like rocks or asphalt) and drop the clams down to shatter their shells. This simple behavior actually requires quite sophisticated thinking because the birds not only need to understand how to utilize gravity, but they must simultaneously connect that to the concept of dense surfaces being more effective in breaking shells than less dense ones like sand. It's a practice they most likely learned through experimentation, which means that birds must have some sort of memory or deductive reasoning. That's impressive considering some people can't open a can with a can opener.

Clams on the Tidal Flats, First Encounter Beach, Eastham.

To survive in this world, you've got to take advantage of whatever abilities you've got and use what you have to make up for what you don't. This first and foremost means recognizing and understanding what you can and can't do. I am what I am, but that doesn't dictate what I can do. I'm not a bird. I cannot fly, but I can learn to use the natural forces to allow me to do it. I am not a clam. I cannot tunnel through the sand but I can develop a thick shell to protect me from those who threaten me. I'm not a crab with sharp claws, but I can learn to be brave like them and face what intimidates me squarely, no matter how big it is.

Clamming is not about speed and strength. It's about precision and strategy. If you scrape your fork just an inch away from the clam, you'll never find it. If you're hasty, you'll pass right over them. If you want to find what you're looking for, you mustn't search haphazardly. It's possible to have a strike of good fortune, but in the end you make your own luck. The more time you spend out there, the better your chances get. You have to methodically look in different places. If you're not in the right place or your searching in the same place over and over, you're just wasting your time.

Of course, success is never guaranteed and a little bit of dumb luck is never a bad thing. Few things in life are a sure thing and the ones that are, like death and change, you can't control. Like the clams, we are just waiting down in the mud to be plucked out of existence at any moment. We can't run from it, we can only hide and prolong the inevitable as long as we can. Our creations, like a clam's shell, live on longer than our bodies, but even those don't last forever.

When clamming, you have to take what you can get. Sometimes the tide comes in and you've barely found a thing. Other times you even go home empty handed. But if you're diligent and go back, you'll fill your bucket in time. There's no need to dig deep. You only have to lightly scratch below the surface. You want to go and return without leaving any permanent traces of your visit, only scratch-marks and footsteps, which get washed away. It's a good philosophy when interacting with nature in general.

If we take all of the clams today, there will be nothing left for tomorrow. That's karma. Take too much and suffer the consequences of your excess. Therefore, we should treat the Earth the way a pennywise millionaire treats their bank account, living off of the interest. It's best not to dip into the principal investment because once you upset the balance and start spending more than you are earning, the money (or the population of clams) quickly runs out. That's why when clamming or fishing you should always leave the little ones. Let them grow and reproduce for the sake of their species and your own future food stock.

It's a fragile balance on the sand flats and that balance can easily become disturbed. I've seen it first-hand. Black muscles used to be incredibly easy to find. You'd find them everywhere lying around in bunches attached to each other by a web of organic filaments. But now muscles aren't so easy to come by. Maybe the population ballooned and died off, or maybe we took too much.

Sadly, red tides (often caused from agricultural run off) are occurring more and more frequently, which temporarily causes the shellfish population to carry bacteria that's dangerous for humans to consume. It's the price we pay for green grass, most of which is not natural and doesn't belong on a place like Cape Cod. If you want to respect the land, don't plant non-native plant species in your yard.

We mustn't bite the hand that feeds us. We have to treat every small part of our world with equal respect. Only this way will we prolong and prosper in our existence. Humans are no better or more important than the tiny clam that lives in the mud. We're just in a different position, although what separates us from clams goes beyond simple anatomy. We humans have the ability to make a conscious choice in what we do, what we eat and how we choose to interact with our environment. With our elevated intelligence, we must accept that we still live in the natural realm of things. We, too, are animals and are just a part of life's mosaic. We mustn't fool ourselves into thinking we are more than that.

Thankfully, the towns on Cape Cod regulate who legally gets access to the bounty of the sea. But what if somebody were to come in and take all of the clams the way the oil barons take fossil fuels from the earth? Who really owns the clams in the sea? Can anybody really claim them? Clams are not meant for us to own. They're meant for us to eat. The entire Earth is fair game for everybody and everything to use. We all have a right to be here.

It's up to each individual to choose how they spend their time and what impact they leave behind. Our collective legacy will be shaped by what kind of world we pass on to posterity. It's basic etiquette to leave a borrowed place, like a rented home, as nice as you found it. For the Earth, that means with fish in the sea and clams in the sand. My hope and prayer is that in two hundred years, people will still be able to do these simple things, like clamming, which I love to do so much. A single individual can't decide the future, but every individual has a hand in shaping it.

Life's truths and rewards are revealed to those who have the courage to search for them even in the dirtiest, smelliest places. Just remember, when you go out looking, you will find something but it won't always be what you were looking for.

Sunset at First Encounter Beach, Eastham.

6 BIKING

The bicycle (like the sailboat) is an ingenious invention, which uses mechanical advantage to amplify a rider's strength, allowing them to travel vast distances by expending less energy than walking. The poetic beauty of biking is that the driving power comes from within. The rider is what gives the bike animation and breathes life into its metal frame. Even though it's an old invention, the low impact cardiovascular workout should be more relevant in our high tech fossil fuel driven world today.

Once again, balance is of utmost importance while biking, and again, this must come from within. You can only find balance with the world when you learn to control yourself. Steering is not so much about moving as it is about shifting your weight. What is weight? It's matter and as Einstein taught us, it's actually energy.

There's no doubt that we hold a small amount of power in this world. We may not have a lot of control when it comes to the exoteric world outside us, but we do when it comes to the esoteric world within. The balance, especially when biking, is so delicate and fragile that the tiniest deviation or bump in the road can cause it and you to be broken.

The uncompromising solidness of the Earth makes its wrath just as fearsome as the fluid seas. When you fall, and you will at some point, you've got to get back up. If the fall is bad enough, it may take some time. But if you're not dead, you're still in the fight. Therefore, cautiousness is crucial and especially so when you're winding through a forest on a narrow strip of pavement full of sand drifts, fallen branches and other unannounced obstacles.

Know when to go fast and when to go slow, not only because of your limited abilities, but because of those of the bicycle as well. The vehicle becomes an extension of you, so you must know it and know it well. You have to be able to feel your own weight and calculate your path ahead as far as you can see. You can't watch what is right below your feet, but must already know what's there based on what you've seen approaching and be constantly scanning, assessing the path and pre-plotting your course accordingly. If a hazard gets below your feet, it's already too late. You can and should look back and check what's behind you from time to time, but only for a moment. It's a life lesson. Acknowledge the past, but stay focused on the future.

Cape Cod offers an extensive array of bike trails after the authorities cleverly converted the old railroad tracks into paved paths for public use. You can ride the "rail trail" for nearly thirty miles uninterrupted and safely access a plethora of territory by bike. I've spent many days cruising the paths and the beauty of the rail trail is that you feel off the grid. You might have to stop for road crossings now and then, but otherwise you and your bike are not a slave to the traffic light.

Biking, unlike driving, always helps me clear my head. The repetitious circular movements make it meditative. After you get warmed up and find a good pace, you reach "the zone," the place where you consciously pay attention to your breathing and the position you're sitting in. You feel your lungs. You feel the oxygen going in and dispersing into your bloodstream. You feel your muscles strain and the sweat droplets dripping out of your skin.

One time when I was in high school, my brother and I decided to bike to Provincetown from Eastham. The interesting part is that for most of the ride, there is no bike path and at one point my brother and I had to bike down the shoulder of Route 6, the busiest and deadliest road on the Cape. Too many bikers have been killed out there in the driving madness and I'm not going to lie, biking on the side of that highway scared the hell out of me. There was only a narrow shoulder and cars were whipping by in both directions. Some of the vehicles passed within mere feet of me, and every second I was riding there I felt as if I was walking hand in hand with death.

In some ways, my fear on the road is more intense than my fear of the ocean. Even if the ocean is so much fiercer, at least the ocean acts somewhat predictably. It always does what it does for a reason. You might not be able to sense certain cataclysmic catastrophes, but you can learn to read the waves and with experience become aware of their physically characteristic behavior.

On the other hand, human beings, especially drivers, are completely unpredictable. How can you trust that the teenage girl who's texting behind the wheel of her daddy's SUV is going to keep in her lane? A driver wields great power and all it took was one mistake by any one of those drivers and I was done for.

Biking down the road, I imagined all those scenarios unfolding. Then my brother, whom I was following, hesitated, looked both ways and crossed the road, turning down a side street. I was not as bold. I stopped and ended up having to wait a while before I crossed. But eventually I ventured my way over and soon we found ourselves biking down hilly side roads traveled by only a few passing cars.

From then on, it became like a chase, me chasing to keep up with my older brother. The hills were killing me. Up and down, up and down, we biked through the steeply graded slopes. Sometimes he'd wait for me at the top and I'd arrive, wheezing and panting, my thighs and calves burning from exertion and as soon as I'd arrive, he'd smile for a moment and be off again, down the hill and off climbing the next one.

My pursuit of him became metaphysical. It was like chasing the white rabbit down the rabbit hole. I was cursing him for his swiftness and persistence, but I didn't give up. If he could do it, so could I. Then suddenly the road just dead-ended. We could see where we needed to go, but could proceed no further. A tidal flat partially filled with water left us with no option but to turn around and go back through all of the hills we'd just passed.

Retracing our path back, we faced a choice, to continue going all the way back to Route 6 or take a random side road and forge on into the unknown. There was no way either of us was going back to Route 6. We would take our chances in the labyrinth rather than face that chaos again. Getting lost is better than dying.

My brother relaxed his pace and we wandered through the hills, cruising through the forest and passing quaint little houses tucked away in the trees. We didn't know exactly where we were but we knew where we were headed. We crested a hill and the view opened up. The curving coastline of the bay stretched out and Pilgrim's monument, still small and far off, stuck out above the buildings of the town.

My exhaustion reached a forte and after that I sort of went numb. My legs throbbed, but strangely enough they didn't really bother me anymore. I had got used to it by then. My butt hurt more than anything else. The seat was killing me, so I stood up and did what I could to take my weight off of it. The struggle transformed from physical to mental. It became about finding the will to keep going and the strength of mind to force my body into doing what it didn't necessarily want to do.

At first, my body protested. My legs cramped and my stomach churned. Then quite magically my internal system underwent some sort of metabolic transformation. It stopped fighting against me and started working with me. The exhaustion transmuted. I got high. My senses became heightened and attuned to every detail. We stopped to rest when we finally made it onto the bike trails around Provincetown, but not for long because it was like my body wanted to keep going.

My muscles were shaking and twitching with excitement, as if their natural state was to be in motion. My legs were asking for more. It's a bit masochistic I know, but I abided and we continued on through the swerving bike trail, which led through a desert-like landscape of sand dunes. The path snaked up and down through the wind blown deposits and at points the asphalt was covered over. Having slipped on sand before, I slowed down and plowed through the drift trying to follow in my brother's fresh tracks.

The trail ended abruptly at a beach abuzz with people and exhaustion made the scene seem surreal. We parked our bikes and sat down on a bench. I had sweat through my clothes, so I took off my shirt and felt the sun shining on my skin. The breeze cooled me and I took a gulp of water to quench what seemed to be an unquenchable thirst. The water flowing down my throat was a welcome relief, so I savored a few sips. The act of drinking when thirsty feels so good. But I didn't indulge too much. I kept my body wanting more.

Sea gulls were squawking and a small surf was washing up onto shore. There was scattered commotion by the people at the beach and a light flutter of children's laughter resounding in the breeze. A few people were flying kites and I looked up to watch their tails fluttering in the wind. A bit like the kites, I was flying high. I knew I couldn't control the environment but I could control myself.

I had biked to the point of exhaustion for no reason other than curiosity and by testing my limits I came to know myself better that day. I felt proud. My brother had motivated me, but I had pushed myself to actually doing it. We all have help and obstacles but we all make the decision if we will accept and overcome them.

Personal responsibility is so much easier to accept during your triumphs than during your defeats. But I learned something important then: with enough drive, you can accomplish big feats, even ones that seemed impractical or improbable at the start. I learned to enjoy taking the side roads even if it takes longer. The highway may be the quickest way, but in the end, it's just a race to the grave. Sometimes it's better to get off the beaten path, even if that means getting lost, because only when you get lost can you be found again.

Seagull at Coast Guard Beach, Eastham.

The journey of life is grueling and hurts along the way. You may want to give up. You might want to stop going. But if you push through those mental and physical barriers, the voyage itself can reach critical mass and take on a life of its own, driving you farther than you ever intended on going. The most important thing is to try. There's no point in taking unneeded risks, but calculated ones are an absolute necessity for progress. Plot a course even if you don't end up following it.

How you get someplace may be as important as where you go, but whom you go with is the most important thing of all. By this, I don't necessarily mean you need to be with another person. One's self can be the best company of all.

When you like who you are, it's not so bad to be alone. So learn to love yourself and if you don't love yourself, then change something, either what you don't like or your opinion because you're stuck with yourself, your body and its limitations. Never define yourself based on what you can't do, but on what you can. In the end, character isn't measured by what you have. It's measured by what you do.

7 KAYAKING

What's nice about kayaking is that you can access places that are virtually impossible to get to any other way. Since you only really need to draw a few inches of water, you can paddle your way up narrow inlets, shallow channels and find yourself in otherwise untouched territory. You can also use kayaks as a tool to get to clams and fish, but I prefer kayaking as a means of exploration, both internal and external.

Kayaking is not an effortless activity. You have to put in a lot of muscle to move yourself around and yet again, balance is of utmost importance, however not so much in the sense of keeping yourself upright. There are many kayaks, which are quite difficult to flip and you'll actually have to fight to turtle them. I'm talking more about a balance in spatial forces, the right versus the left. Your arms have to work separately to form a collective unit. It's about collaboration. To go straight, the forces exerted by both arms must be in balance. To turn, you have to paddle harder or softer using one arm. If you want to go left, you have to paddle harder with your right or use the left paddle to create drag to help you maneuver more drastically. Overall, the trick to kayaking (and living) is being smooth.

Each action has to be guided intentionally. Flailing is a useless activity, which needlessly expends energy and makes you tire out more quickly. The secret is to feel the flow and move fluidly like the water you're navigating in. Water offers both friction and flow. Once you build up inertia, it becomes easier to paddle. Acceleration is what uses up the most energy. So you want to try to keep your speed steady.

When kayaking, environmental conditions are again a large factor in your day. The wind plays a part, since your body sits above the kayak and acts like a small sail. It can provide you with an added boost or perpetual resistance. Since often times you are going to make a loop and ultimately return back to the same place you set out from, you're usually going to have to fight the wind in at least one direction. If the wind is at your side, it can be equally annoying as it forces you to position yourself at an angle to your forward motion, which increases your drag.

However, the power of the wind on you is nothing compared to the tide. Fighting against the tide is sometimes impossible. If you're stuck in an inlet, it's like trying to paddle up a swiftly flowing river. This is particularly evident in narrow channels where the moving water gets bottlenecked. In many locations, the tide can even leave you high and dry, so you have to be careful where you paddle when the water's high, because your passage way back might disappear before your eyes. I've had to drag my kayak a good distance quite a few times and trust me it's a lot easier to paddle the kayak in water than it is to drag it over sand. But that sort of thing is bound to happen during exploration. Mishaps and miscalculations are how you learn and what kayaking has really taught me is about my place in the flow of energy.

The water of the tides is moving independently from me. For all practical purposes, I have absolutely no effect on its behavior. I can try all I want to stop and contain the water, but it is going to keep going in the direction it naturally wants to travel (toward bodies of mass, like the moon and the sun). To me, that force is a god, since it's power cannot be reckoned with.

You can't control the tide, but you can learn to predict and anticipate it. A day of kayaking can be made or broken by choosing when and where you drop in. Realistically, there are few ideal times when you can calculate to go out and in traveling with the tide after it switches. Most days it's a balancing act when choosing your location and time. The tide moves differently in different places. In inlets, for example, all of the water is moving out to sea, but that doesn't mean it will do so in a straight line. Depending on the orientation of sandbars, there are places where the water flows directly away from the open ocean.

Exploration should be guided by that natural flow, but as they say, "only dead fish travel with the flow." Therefore, you must use the flow to your advantage when you can but you can't avoid fighting it forever. Sometimes you have to paddle against the current to get to where you want to go. That's something both philosophical and practical.

Socially, the best leaders are people who can't only see the changing tides, but have the willpower to fight against them and anticipate their changes. If you always go with the flow of the tide, you'll be stuck in a constant circle, going out and coming back in, ultimately traveling nowhere at all. To break out of that cycle, you have to fight. No progress comes without resistance and this doesn't only apply to social change. It applies to personal change as well.

Kayaking in Nauset Marsh, Eastham.

All of our habits and daily behaviors lead to a cyclical flow of energy. Like the tides, you may not be able to control them, but you can learn to use them and to have the strength and knowledge to be able to effectively fight them on occasion. The tides may influence our lives, but they need not dictate them. So kayaking is not only a physical exercise, it's an exercise in free will and autonomy. Freedom demands a constant fight and is only possessed by those who struggle to stay free and exercise their right to it.

It's not easy to fight against the flow and travel forward if the wind is also blowing in your face. When the elements line up against you, the lack of control is sobering. You realize that you're just a drop of water in an ocean, a speck of dust living on a speck of dust, which is orbiting around a slightly bigger burning speck of dust. The world is infinitely small and infinitely big. Size matters, but only in what you are up against. To a bacterium, I am an inconceivably large and complicated giant. But to the Earth, I'm an inconsequentially small grain of sand.

One of the most fatal mistakes that people sometimes make is fooling themselves into believing they are bigger than they are. It's delusional to think you hold great sway in this world, even if you're an emperor, a prince, a CEO, a queen or a president. It doesn't matter if your face is on a coin or your likeness has been carved into stone. When the Earth moves, you move with it. When the tide turns, it takes another six hours before it will start coming back. If you realize, recognize and consciously acknowledge this basic fact, you'll save yourself a lot of trouble. Some people call it opening up to "God," but I find it unnecessary to use such narrowing labels. To me, it is more like accepting the fundamental truths.

You can equip yourself and plan accordingly, but as always, there's no such thing as a sure thing. You never know what is going to get in your way and you can't always be prepared to meet it. But if you learn to anticipate things, you might be able to head off problems and prevent yourself from getting into a bad situation beforehand. Neglect the mighty forces at your own peril. If you don't recognize the true nature of things, then you'll forever be frustrated and paddling against the whims of the tide.

8 SHOPPING

Shopping is another activity that triggers our natural instincts but in a less physical way. Shopping is sometimes as much about the idea of acquiring the product as it is about possessing the item itself. In other words, the act of shopping can bring you more joy than what you've bought. But shopping is not about just finding whatever you're searching for. It's about looking, and browsing can be fun.

In many ways, shopping triggers our natural instinct to pursue resources. Since the beginning of our existence, humans have traveled far and wide all around the globe and most of that exploration was driven as much by necessity as it was by curiosity. In the deserts of Africa, we had to find water and chase herds of animals into unknown territories. Then there's always been the search for a suitable mate to reproduce with. The ones who had the skills to find those things were the ones that survived and passed on their genes. So shopping can actually be thought of as a combination of the traditionally masculine trait of pursuit with the feminine urge for selection.

Shopping for something you need is elementary. You buy what you must: food, water and utilities. Shopping for what you don't need is more advanced, because you buy what you can. It's about desire and choice. Like when choosing a mate, you shouldn't merely take what you can get. Sometimes, there is a bargain, which you must snatch up. Otherwise, when making a big purchase, you've got to do some shopping around first. There are a lot of fish in the sea, just like there are a lot of stores on the Cape.

We may call it bargain hunting, but to me, it's more like foraging and what makes shopping on Cape Cod so interesting is that there are so many unique and different things to be found. It's an artistic haven and unlike most malls, where items are standard and can be re-stocked, there are many treasures on Cape Cod that can only be found there. Sometimes, they're native, other times they drift in from cultural currents elsewhere.

No place is this more evident than at a flea market. Flea markets are not only great places to pick up name brand seconds, but they also offer a variety of products that can't be easily categorized. Go to a flea market and you'll quickly see the newest trends in art and fashion. The range of its products spans from recently released electronics to antique furniture. Some vendors are backed by commercial businesses, but most are just individuals selling knock-offs and seconds (clothing and products which have flaws and cannot be sold in retail stores at full price). There are also many people, who just sit there and sell their old junk.

The truth is that most of the stuff being sold at flea markets (and everywhere for that matter) is junk, whether it's old or new. Nowadays, so many products are only made to be thrown out and serve no other purpose than moving a buck from one hand to another. After that one transaction takes place, the item goes straight into the landfill, where it sits and rots for who knows how long. But sometimes in the flea market hiding amongst all of that junk is a gem, something of true value and substance.

When I was younger I went for the toys and sports cards, but as I've aged I've begun to embrace the antiques. It all started one day when I found a book. There was a man at the flea market selling a variety of household items, like an estate sale. Amidst the random appliances and domestic accessories was a crate full of hard cover books. I was scanning through the titles when one of the names caught my eye. "Classic American Folk Songs."

I opened up the crisp barely ever before turned pages and beheld an entire book full of sheet music. I plopped down on the pavement and began leafing through the hundred pages one by one. Then I looked at the index and through the arrangement of melodies. I fell in love and was fully intending on buying it, but didn't have any money on me, so I had to go find my parents. Without thinking, I got up, put the book back and began walking away when I heard a man's voice address me.

"You like books huh?" He asked.

"Yeah." I answered, once I realized he was talking to me.

"Here." The man said, handing me the book with a smile. "I can see you like books. I like books too. Take it."

"Thanks." I beamed without hesitation.

Over the next months, I studied every one of the melodies in that book and don't know how many times I've played them all. It aided me greatly in my studies and started me down a musical path. The gift was a bit mystical really, almost like the man was a prophet which had bestowed the book upon me, like a sign or whatever you want to call it. Fate. Somehow, he knew I would use it. He understood me without knowing me. He knew the book belonged in my hands, because I would protect it, cherish it and ultimately pass it on. I still have that book and use it.

After that day, I started looking through flea markets a lot more carefully. It was my first find and it was glorious. That was sweet, but likewise shopping can also be sour and I can still vividly remember my first loss. Sometimes, I still kick myself for passing up the offer.

As a musician, I always search for instruments and one time I found a beat up old guitar. It wasn't like the other cheap guitars I usually found sitting out in the sun. It was a Gibson (essentially the Mustang of guitars) hollow body acoustic, which means it was about the size of a regular acoustic guitar, only a little bit thinner and instead of having a single central sound hole under the strings, like most acoustic guitars, it had two sound holes shaped like those of a violin.

I picked up the treasure and looked at it. It was beaten up, broken and overall in sad shape. The neck was dinged up and partially separated from the body. It looked nice, but also pretty badly cared for.

"How much?" I asked the woman.

"Two fifty." She answered. "But I'll give it to you for two twenty five."

"No thanks." I said shocked and walked away.

At the time I thought she was crazy for asking so much for a beat up and broken guitar. I knew nothing back then but a couple of years later saw a similar guitar for sale in a music shop. The guitar was being sold for almost three thousand dollars. I don't know if it was exactly the same model, but I realized that the guitar I had been looking at was most likely built in the 70's or even the 60's and was a vintage classic.

I could have easily bought it for two hundred and twenty-five dollars, spent five hundred fixing it up and ended up with a one of a kind instrument worth more than any monetary value you can place on it. It's the kind of guitar you don't sell. It's one a pro plays and treats kindly, like a good woman. For me, it was the one that got away and sometimes late at night, I still lay in bed and think of that guitar and wonder what could have been. I've spent many days at the flea market looking for it, hoping to see it again, but an opportunity like that only comes along once in a lifetime if you're lucky.

I was young and foolish, and I've tried to learn from my mistake. Hesitating can be lethal. In communication you can say more by a hesitation than you can by actually speaking. You can tell almost as much about a person by their inactions as you can by their actions. Reading people is important, especially when bartering.

Bartering is like playing a game of poker. You have to be able to bluff and make the seller believe your interested but that you don't really want to buy the item as much as you really do. Once the salesperson sees you want it, he'll see you're bluffing and attack. In a flea market, the price isn't always written on the item, so you often have to ask how much it costs. Not labeling things saves on work, but it also gives the salesperson some flexibility and the opportunity to size up a potential customer.

A good salesperson is ruthless and will turn the situation around on you. They'll make you fight for what you want to buy from them. But in the end, its not about how much money you pay, it's about what you get in return. The goal is to spend a fair amount of money, given what the item means to you and what the money and loss of inventory means to the salesperson.

Most times, the buyer loses. Let's face it. In the corporate capitalist culture, where profit is often the sole driving factor, it's all about essentially screwing the consumer. A truly "good" company is one that produces a product with a vision beyond the sale of it. A truly "good" product is one that is useful and reliable beyond its monetary value, is more than its parts and should be able to be fixed.

However, these types of products are not always as profitable as ones that easily break and are impossible to fix. You can all too conveniently buy an item, which is cheap and at the time of purchase appears to be a good deal. But you're really just getting ripped off. The world is filled with crap and excessiveness, which we don't need. Shopping is the act and process of discovering the things you truly want and need. You give your time to get money and use your money to buy things. So ultimately, you should be careful how you spend your time and money.

There's a cheap thrill in finding a bargain basement deal or something you really wanted to buy and would've paid a lot more to purchase. It makes you feel good. It's like stealing but without the guilt. It's finding something by chance and of course involves some luck. However, always remember, "caveat emptor" or "buyer beware." Many items are not as good, cool or useful as they seem to be. Quantity, quality and utility are relative terms. Consistency can be questionable and something never comes for nothing. It is a law of physics that every force produces an equal and opposite force. You could say the same for shopping.

What you buy determines where the money goes and what the resources are used for. In many ways, what you buy even dictates who you are and what you are in society. Some people live and find joy in paying a lot, some by paying a little. Ultimately, it's not about the price tag on the item or where you bought it, it's about the item itself. If you buy a two hundred dollar pair of jeans and never wear them, then you've wasted your money, but if you buy the same pair of jeans and wear them everyday for two years, it's actually more cost efficient than buying a cheap ten-dollar pair of jeans and only wearing them once.

Like all of the other activities I've talked about, shopping can also be addictive like a drug, which you just can't seem to get enough of. So you have to watch yourself and always be aware of what you're buying. Sometimes you buy just to buy and that's exactly what a good capitalist should be doing to keep the engine of the economy moving. Money is a resource, which is meant to be used. But be wise with your spending. A healthy government and a healthy household is one that is balanced with the money it is taking in and the money it is spending.

Shopping can become like a disease if you spend more than you are taking in. So each purchase should be looked at as an investment. First buy what you need, then buy what you want. The most important thing is to know yourself, know what you want and what you need. Of course, in our modern material world, it's become quite difficult to tell the difference between the two, but in truth all you really need is food, water and shelter. I won't narrow myself to saying that all food, water and shelter are the same. The food should be healthy, the water should be clean, and the shelter should be adequate for whatever climate you are living in. What you want, that's a completely different story.

What do I want? What do I really want? Those are questions you should ask yourself often, especially when you're shopping. If you've got some extra cash and it's burning a hole in your pocket, anything can seem good, particularly if it's cheap. It's ok to indulge yourself from time to time on something pointless and expendable, but if you want get more bang for your buck, you've got to be reserved and do your research.

Cape Cod offers so many unique and interesting items that you can easily spend all your money in one place if you're not careful, so self-control is essential. You have to look around first before you can understand what you really want. How do you know you really want it? I don't know. How do you know when you're in love? You just do. I don't mean to equate love with purchasing, but they're both about where your priorities are and what you value.

All in all, the best part about life and shopping on Cape Cod is that it's unexpected. You never know what the weather is going to be like or what you're going to find. The best gets, like the best days, are often the unplanned ones, the things you find by accident, when you're not even looking for them. You might go out looking for a new pair of sunglasses and come back with a tide clock.

You never know what's out there and that's why you keep looking. I'm still waiting for that vintage Gibson guitar or an early printing of "Moby Dick" signed by Herman Melville. I'm not sure if I'll ever find one, but I'll keep my eyes open and keep on looking. In the meantime, I'll try not to waste too much of my money on junk because I want to be ready and have enough just in case I ever find one of those gems again.

9 COOKING AND EATING

Hunger and thirst are our most basic desires after breathing. They're even more primal than sex. We'll fight to mate, but we'll kill to eat. I'm not a monk, so for me, eating is an act that should be enjoyed. It's a simple luxury, which can bring pleasure, so the type of eating I'm talking about goes beyond our fundamental need to do it. I'm talking about the experience of eating something extraordinary.

There are numerous top-notch restaurants and clam shacks scattered all throughout the Cape and picking your restaurant is a lot like picking your surfing or fishing spot. You've got to go where works for you. Each day brings a different hunger and a different yearning, so different foods might suit you depending on your appetite. Again, awareness is everything. You have to know your tastes and your body, what types of foods make you feel good and what bothers you. For this reason, always be careful of what and how much you eat because eating is also like a drug and it helps to keep at least a loose leash on your desire.

Part of taste has to do with personal preference, but it also has to do with our level of hunger. It takes three key factors for food to taste great. First, the ingredients have to be fresh. Second, it has to be prepared properly and third (this is a big AND) you must be hungry.

Proper preparation doesn't mean complex or complicated. Some of the best foods are prepared in the simplest ways. In fact, you can easily destroy the positive qualities of food by cooking it the wrong way. Likewise, if you're not hungry, even the best food doesn't taste all that great. Therefore, eating depends very much on your hunger. You have to find the right food to fit your taste and mood at the time you're eating it. What you fancy is up to you whether it's fast food or five-star cuisine.

In my opinion, even though it's nice to go out to dinner and have your food prepared by professionals, cooking your own meal can be just as gratifying as eating itself, especially when you're cooking fish you've harvested from the sea by hand (which is also a great way to work up an appetite, as is surfing, biking, kayaking etc.).

Cooking is all about chemistry, so like with most everything in life, you have to find a balance by cooking the food just enough, but not too much, and at the right temperature for the right amount of time. Whether you're talking about steak or pasta, over-cooking can be just as tragic, if not more, than under-cooking because at least if you undercook something, you can always salvage it by putting it on for a bit longer. Once you cook something you can't un-cook it. You can't go back in time. What's done is done and what's overdone is overdone. This is especially true with fish.

Fish generally cooks faster than meat because of its protein structure and unless you're cooking a soup or a stew, overcooking fish is one of the worst things you can do to it because it ruins the fish's texture and flavor, and even destroys some of its healthy properties. You already killed it once. There's no need to kill it again. That's why you have to develop a sense for cooking fish and this is usually accomplished through experience.

Like surfing and sailing, cooking changes under different conditions and takes a lot of trial and error to do correctly. You have to feel the food you're cooking and give it your full attention, because how you interact with the food affects how it tastes. Preparing a meal can also be a meditative practice and provides a good time for reflection. Also, like fishing, it gives you an intimate relationship with what you consume as you get to see directly what goes into what you eat and watch the raw products turn into a feast.

So, for the sake of all, I am going to divulge some basic and simple cooking tips, which were passed on to me, and which I hope will help others to properly and fully enjoy the bounty of the sea.

First off: lobster. It's expensive and it should be. They might look like bugs and technically they're not far off from insects on the tree of life, but lobsters get big and therefore take quite some time to mature. The average lifespan of a lobster is roughly fifty years. The largest lobster ever caught was over 44 pounds and about a meter long! That means the average 1.5 to 2 pound lobster you find in the market is around 5-7 years old, so lobsters take almost as much time as people do to mature. Therefore, like a fine wine, lobsters are a delicacy and should be treated as such. (Then again, so should all living things, big and small.)

Many restaurants have a tendency to overcook lobster, mostly because of health codes, but it's also tricky to properly cook lobster because of its anatomy and the chef's inability to test the meat inside to see when it's done. However, there is a simple and easy way for anybody to accurately and consistently cook lobster, no matter what size it is. *Note: the following method is meant for sea level elevation. In high altitudes, where water boils at a lower temperature, more time is needed. But I'm not talking about eating lobster in the mountains. I'm talking about eating lobster near the sea.

First off, you have to have a pot of water, which is proportional to the size of the lobster being cooked in it. In other words, the lobster or lobsters should be able to fit completely and comfortably immersed inside the water. Once you get the water to a rolling boil, drop the lobsters in headfirst and use a cover. Do it fast and then (this is also very important) hold the cover down for a good twenty to thirty seconds as upon their death, the lobsters might twitch and kick around boiling water. It's morbid. I know, a terribly cruel fate. But dropping the lobsters in headfirst to water already boiling ensures their death is rather quick.

Now here is the real important information, the formula to calculate how long you need to cook the lobsters. My father acquired this recipe from an old salt up in Canada and it goes like this: ten minutes for the first pound and two minutes for every pound after that. Read it again. That's ten minutes for the first pound and two minutes for every pound after. So...if you have a one-pound lobster, you simply cook it for ten minutes since the first pound gets ten minutes. (Note: You shouldn't be eating any lobsters much smaller than this, as it's against the law for conservation purposes). But if you have a two-pound lobster, you cook it for twelve minutes, ten minutes for the first pound and two minutes for the second (10 + 2). If you have a three-pound lobster, you cook it for fourteen minutes (10 + 2 + 2). If you have a five-pound lobster you cook it for eighteen minutes (10 + 2 + 2 + 2 + 2).

You can also split the two's in half to calculate more accurately for oddly sized lobsters. Say you have a two and a half-pound lobster, you cook it for thirteen minutes. (10 + 2 + 1). If you have multiple lobsters, DO NOT add up their poundage for the time. Treat both lobsters as individuals. If you have a one-pound and two pound lobster you cook the one-pounder for ten minutes and the two-pounder for twelve. You can smoothly do this in the same pot by putting in the two-pound lobster two minutes before the one-pounder. The most important thing is to keep the water at a rolling boil. If you do that, it works like a charm every time and yields perfectly tender claw and tail meat.

There is no way to cook every part of the lobster uniformly because of its anatomy. Therefore, certain parts, like the "fingers" of the claw and the tips of the tail where the meat is thin, will always end up being more cooked than the thicker meat of the tail. But the formula ensures the entire lobster gets fully cooked without being over-cooked.

Each part of a lobster tastes different so part of the beauty of eating lobster is that there is so much variation, and to me, the part of the lobster you like can be used to define your personality in some ways. It's like being a boob guy or a butt guy. Do you like the claws or the tail? Some people like very particular places, for instance the "arm" which attaches the claws or the little legs, which are a bit stringier, like crab. The meat varies greatly in texture and taste throughout and deep inside are some hidden treasures particularly in the sockets of the appendages, which offer extremely sweet but only bite sized morsels. They're often tiny in small lobsters and you might get only one or two bites for all of the work dissecting the lobster, but it's worth it. The rarity only increases its splendor.

Personally, I like all of the parts of the lobster in their own way. I'm not a huge fan of the eggs and not because they're eggs, but because I don't like the texture. The same goes for the innards. Yes, eating lobster can be gross, but so is life. You have to dig in and break through the spiky exterior to get to the sweet center. You have to fight and sometimes you bleed (because seriously you can get cut up on the shell), but that's all part of the game and it's a small price to pay for such a fulfilling reward.

Some people find it unbearable. They don't want to think about what they're eating, but if you can get beyond that queasy feeling and embrace the animal in you, you can dive in with no fear and enjoy it even more. Part of the fun of eating lobster is getting dirty and it's impossible not to when you're ripping through a fluid filled carcass. It's barbaric and primal, but uncompromisingly real. Life itself is disgusting, slimy and filled with a disturbing amount of detail, which can be overwhelming. But you have no choice. That's life. You can either get used to looking at it or spend your life looking away from it.

Whereas with lobsters you dig through their defenses and eat some parts inside, when eating clams you devour their entire body whole, everything at once. If you want to go "au natural," the best way to eat little necks (quahogs) and oysters is raw. Like with lobster, you'll have to fight your way in and opening up raw clams is tricky business. I've cut myself a number of times on broken shells and slipping knives, so I wouldn't recommend trying to open clams raw unless you know what you're doing.

The process of opening a raw clam is really a bit like picking a lock. It helps to cool them down in the fridge first as it relaxes their muscles. Even then, once the clam realizes you're trying to get in, it'll clamp up and fight to the death. Your job is to force your blade through the small divide in its shell and slice the muscle that connects the clam. Once the muscle is severed, the clam (or oyster) will pop right open and you can scrape the rest of its body off of the shell.

There are certain risks when eating raw shellfish, like rare food-born diseases but hey, that's life. Everything is dangerous in a way. The main rule with clams and seafood in general is to get them fresh. This way whatever bacteria and pathogens may be lurking around don't have time to populate. The optimal way to consume any fish is immediately after it dies and even the clams you buy in the store should still be alive when you buy them. The key is don't eat anything that smells bad. Now I understand that smell can be relative and that some people might find the aroma of fish gross in general, but there's a difference. If it smells like the ocean and the beach, it's fine. That's normal and what it should smell like. But if it smells like old socks and makes you gag, don't eat it.

Fresh raw clams go down easily and leave you feeling great afterwards. It's like you can feel their life-energy being sucked directly into your bloodstream as the nutrients of their body are quickly absorbed into yours. Something about it makes me feel like it's the way people are meant to eat and I'm sure it rings true to some extent, as we evolved for millions of years without cooked food. Only rather recently in our evolutionary history did humans begin preparing food so eloquently. What change has this made in our lives? A big one.

Cooking offers a clear advantage as it sterilizes the food and decreases the likelihood of ingesting and passing on malignant pathogens. Unfortunately, humans have lost balance and nowadays we cook and prepare food in ways that actually increase our risk of long-term health problems. During our evolution we didn't have to worry so much about the long term, now we do.

Most seafood in itself is extremely healthy and offers great benefits to you as a part of your diet. However, when you deep-fry those healthy unsaturated fats in oil, it can counteract many of those healthy benefits. I'm not going to knock it. It's good. Fried clams and fish and chips are great. I love to eat them when everything is fresh and fried just right. But it makes the food a bit plastic. Granted sometimes plastic is good, it can be helpful and convenient, but it's not the kind of thing you want to eat every day. The healthiest and for me the best way to cook clams is to steam them.

Steamers (or long neck clams) are by far the sweetest, but muscles and quahogs are tasty as well. Like lobster, how long you cook a clam depends on its size. So the only way to cook clams reliably is to watch them closely. They're done when they completely open up. Cooking time varies relative to many factors both within the clam (shell thickness, size etc.) and how close the clam is to the heat source. Therefore, I'll divulge a good way to cook quahogs consistently by using only a frying pan.

Fill the frying pan with about a half an inch of water, place it on the stove and then carefully stand up the quahogs one by one by balancing them on the hinge of their shell. It's a bit like setting up dominoes and you must have a smooth hand because you can easily knock them all down just by touching one. Once you have them standing, bring the water to a boil and watch. You can tell when they're done because they suddenly pop open. As soon as you see the transformation, take the individual out.

The more you cook anything, the more you break down its chemical structure. To get the full benefit of any food you're eating, you want to maintain that structure as much as possible. That's why you want to remove the clams as soon as they finish cooking all the way through. This way they'll be moist and tender, not tough and chewy. Sometimes I wonder if many people don't like seafood simply because they've had it served badly once or twice and have developed negative associations with it.

When cooking fish you have some options: baked, grilled or pan-fried are just a few. They all offer their own strength and hassle, so it depends on what you like and what type of fish you're cooking. Striped bass, cod and haddock go well in pretty much any form since they're white fish and have a mild flavor. Bluefish are a little bit more finicky to cook, because they have darker meat and a stronger taste. Bluefish are extremely rich in nutrients and vitamins, but they can get a little heavy at times, especially if the fish is big. So for me, the best way to cook bluefish is on the grill because grilling helps to lighten it up by draining out and burning most of the oil. Another one of my favorite ways to eat bluefish is smoked because that's when all of the subtle flavors really come out but still, it's quite rich and impossible to do unless you have all the equipment.

One time I caught a blue and ran out of propane when I was heating up the grill. I had to do something and I had to do it fast. The fish was all filleted and ready to go, so I improvised. In a flash, an idea struck me: blackened blue fish. In theory, it sounded perfect. So I went to the Internet and quickly looked up a reference guide on how to "blacken" a fish entrée. I heated up a pan, salted it and tossed on a filet.

It started smoking immediately, like it's supposed to, so I opened up the windows and rode it out. I seared both sides thoroughly and when I felt it was ready, I pulled it off and walked outside because the kitchen was clouded with a haze. The result was actually quite tasty and I was pleasantly surprised by my experiment because much of the fish's oil had been released and gone up in smoke, so the meat wasn't so dense and the outside had a light black crisp, which gave it a little crunch. The consistency inside was warm and tender and truthfully I would really like to cook it more often that way. The only problem is that it made a great mess and left the kitchen reeking of smoky bluefish for the next few days.

There are so many different ways to cook fish, but a general rule of thumb is to cook the fish just to the point where the segments of the fish easily slide apart. Use a fork to push it. If it's fully cooked it will give and the skin will just slip off. After that happens at the largest part of the filet the fish is done and you should shut off the heat. From that point on, you're over cooking it, so remove the fish from whatever source of heat you're using, whether it's in the oven or on the grill.

Again, no matter what type of fish it is, the most important thing is that it is fresh (or freshly flash-frozen). It's the most critical aspect of how the fish will taste. You can't really make something that's bad taste good. Our senses may not be perfect, but they're pretty good and tough to fool. Even if you cook old fish perfectly, it's still going to taste like old fish.

There's no way of getting around it. Seafood has a short shelf life and offers a great little lesson on life's impermanence. Seafood is something that can't easily be stockpiled, unless it's arduously cured, otherwise there's no use in saving it. The lesson is that there's no point in hoarding too much and taking more than you can consume. The distribution of fish could even provide a quick lesson on economics because fish, like many products, quickly loses its value and potential worth. In my opinion, canned foods and preservatives are not only perverting our eating habits and leading to an imbalanced lifestyle, they are also straining our society by creating vast differences in wealth distribution and equality.

I love eating. I love the act of eating. It feels good and part of that joy comes from our temporary release from hunger. But we all eat only to become hungry again. We're stuck in that karmic circle and there's really no way to escape it. We have to eat, so we might as well enjoy it. But like everything, we shouldn't lose our heads. We too may be animals, but part of the reason humans act differently and are different from other animals is that we can exhibit conscious self-control. We might not have the ability to completely escape our instincts, but we need not be slaves to them. So know what to eat, when to eat and how to eat.

If you exercise, you'll need to eat more, so if you love eating, you can easily use exercise as a means of indulging yourself, the same way if you love spending money, you can use working as a means to go shopping. It's tension and release, constantly, with everything, for our whole lives, a cycle, like the seasons and the days.

Maybe it's a bit masochistic to consciously deprive yourself and push your body, but I also believe it's ascetic. Not giving yourself something for a period of time makes you appreciate it more and understand its place in your life. Abstinence can be a good thing, but not when taken to an extreme, nothing is. It's good to have some self-control and self-discipline, but you cannot completely ignore the beast. The animal in us must be satisfied, so when you're thirsty, drink. When you're hungry, eat and when you're curious, taste. Curiosity is a prerequisite to finding new things. Habit is nice, but sometimes you have to change it up and add a little spice.

It's great to cook and eat with other people but sometimes it's good to do alone. Either way, cooking and eating hold your focus and release your mind for a while. There are three basic needs and one of them is to eat. We have no choice over that, so don't rush it, embrace it. Use eating as an opportunity to relax and take your time. Literally, chew your food. It's better for digestion, taste and helps you avoid choking. But figuratively, watch out what you eat, because in the end it becomes who you are.

10 SLEEPING AND DREAMING

If you allow yourself to really relax, Cape Cod can give you some needed time to catch up on sleep and get some good "z's." On big wave days, I can hear the waves from the beach at my house and it's the best aid in helping me to fall into a deep sleep. Like the sound of a steady wind in the trees or rain falling, the white noise is relaxing, probably because it reminds us of when we were in the womb.

Sleep is "a little death" and death is "the big sleep" because in both instances, our bodies become vacant of our conscious selves and we become uncommunicative and unresponsive to the outside world. Where do we go when we die? That's a mystery. Where do we go when we sleep? Someplace else, to a world inside and often to our dreams.

I've had some of my most wonderful fantasies either while sleeping on Cape Cod or dreaming about Cape Cod. Likewise, I've also experienced some of my worst nightmares there. Dreams can seem as real as reality and to our consciousness, we perceive dreams the same way we perceive our waking life, so metaphysically speaking our dreams are just as real as the external world during the time we are dreaming.

When you wake up from a bad dream and find yourself in a good place, it's a most wonderful surprise and when you wake up from a good dream in a good place…well, that's not so bad either. Even if I didn't get to finish my fantasy, at least I can go to the beach and let reality sort things out. Waking up from a fantasy can be disappointing, but the Cape gives you some consolation. You might not get your dream life, but at least you're alive and get to experience something like it, if only for a time.

Dunes at White Crest Beach, Wellfleet.

I've had many dreams about surfing and fishing on the Cape and I've even had some about shopping and cooking. I often dream about waves and sometimes the beach gets transformed into a surreal place. I've talked to John Lennon, Jesus and the Dalai Lama on the dunes of the Cape. I've built giant sandcastles in my dreams and ridden the perfect wave, truly wonderful scenes. But I've also seen some terrible misfortunes, the likes of which I cannot erase from my brain.

Sometimes I see sharks in the water and once I even watched a great white come out of the sea and devour a young boy, who was playing at the water's edge. I could see the shark coming and was screaming for the boy to get out of the way, but the young boy remained unaware until it was too late. In a flash, he was gone and all I could see was the tail of the shark swimming away. The image is still burned in my head and the feeling of absolute dread and emptiness still makes my stomach churn. What does it mean? That's a tough question to answer.

I'm not sure who the boy was. Maybe it was I. Maybe the shark represents the dangers of the world and the boy represents innocence and my inability to do anything to control it. Dreams have patterns and reoccurring themes. I often dream about being on a beach that has perfect waves, but find myself without a surfboard, at times when I'm no doubt mentally frustrated and can't have something I desire.

It's good to analyze your dreams because they give you a window of insight into your subconscious and can tell you things about your psyche, which you might not always like to confess consciously. But don't look too deeply into them or you might miss the point. For instance, maybe the shark and the boy don't represent anything. Maybe the shark is a shark and I'm merely projecting my fear of them into my dreams.

We spend much of our lives asleep and essentially in another state of consciousness. But what is sleep? Nobody really knows its exact purpose, but it seems to be essential for resting our conscious mind. The body doesn't actually sleep when we are sleeping. Our heart is still beating, our blood is still flowing and our lungs are still breathing. In fact our body remains actively awake for most of our sleep, especially when we're dreaming.

The key to dreaming is sleeping. You've got to get into a particular stage of the sleep cycle in order to dream. Not all sleep is equal. Only a deep sleep is truly restful and most of our dreams never enter our conscious minds. We forget them immediately after we experience them. It's usually only when we awake during a dream that we can consciously recall it, but who knows about the dreams we see, but don't remember and how much they affect our moods.

Even though dreams only last mere minutes, they seem to go on for hours. That's because while we are sleeping, we step outside of the "real" universe and into a somewhat timeless physical non-existence. A sleeping person wakes up for the most part unaware of how long they've been sleeping.

Eating well and exercising usually help you sleep more soundly, so there are things you can do while you're awake to help you sleep. Maybe that's why I seem to sleep so well after a long day at the beach and even on the beach.

Sleeping on the beach in the sand feels so organic. Close your eyes and you can hear the gentle sloshing of the water on the sand, the calls of seagulls off in the distance and feel the gentle breeze blowing through your hair, as the sun warmly kisses your skin. Just beware because falling asleep on the beach can be dangerous in the middle of the day. Make sure you cover your skin and apply plenty of sunscreen or you'll wake up as red as a lobster.

The ocean has a way of relaxing and lulling you to sleep. It invites you to fade away to another place, underneath the surface of reality we see everyday. Maybe it's the sound or maybe it's the smell, but mostly I think it's the energy the ocean emits. It pulls you in, draws you near and washes all of your problems away. Sleep gives you a release, freeing your mind and as the Cape can be an escape from stress, so can sleep.

11 PLAYING IN THE SAND

Playing in the sand as a child taught me one of life's most important lessons, which I've already touched upon briefly, impermanence. By definition, "impermanence" is the state of being impermanent, and "impermanent" is defined as "not permanent," with "permanent" meaning, "continuing or enduring without fundamental or marked change." Therefore, in laymen's terms, nothing that "is" will remain the same. At first, this truth can be quite sad and unsettling.

When I was young I would spend a lot of time carefully building a castle in the sand only to have it fall down because of the wind or the waves or someone else coming and knocking it down. Organized entities are so difficult to create and so easy to destroy. A tree that takes a hundred years to grow can be cut down in a minute. Hair that takes a lifetime to groom is gone with a single snip. Once done, these things cannot be undone. Nothing can.

The beach is like an empty canvass, which you can write on, but at the end of the day the canvass always gets wiped clean. Fighting against it is fruitless. The only thing you can do is to accept it and once you do, the impermanence isn't so frightening. It can even be liberating.

Sometimes I enjoy destroying my sand creations as much as I love creating them. After all, destruction and decomposition are as important to development as death is to life. Death not only feeds growth, it clears the way for the next generations and destruction itself can be counter-intuitively productive by creating space for new creation. Think of it this way, if all of the sandcastles we ever made never fell down, then there'd be no place to build any more. What goes up must come down. Decay is as important as growth. You can't say one is good or the other is bad. They just are. They are two sides of a coin, the mountain and the valley and the two-halves form a full circle. These circular cycles are everywhere: Night and day, summer and winter, high tide and low tide, life and death. We cannot have one without the other. Only together is the circle complete.

We can build out of steel and concrete, which seems strong, but in the grand scheme of things, it's really no different than sand. They're all just as fragile to the great forces. In the long run, stone turns to sand. Bricks turn to dust. Wood burns. Metal rusts and corrodes. These things don't disappear. They simply change form and move with the natural flow of things to a more disorganized state. But just because nothing lasts forever, doesn't mean it's worthless or unimportant.

A tiny grain of sand seems almost like nothing within itself, but millions of them together form a vast expanse of beach, which can defy the mighty sea. Each piece adds up. They may be small, but they still count. You can think the same way about people.

My father once told me a story, probably a fable, about a storm beaching schools of fish on a tidal flat. Thousands upon thousands of fish lay dying in the sun on the beach and there's an old man, who's working feverishly throwing as many of fish as he can back into the water. A young man comes by and scorns the old man as if he's crazy and says,

"Why bother? You'll never be able to save them all. It doesn't matter what you're doing." To which the old man replies,

"I know I can't save them all, but I'll save as many as I can…and it does matter. It matters greatly to each one of the fish I do save."

The moral of the story is that each action, like a grain of sand, by itself may seem insignificant, but when piled up together form something big, your life. As the world shapes you, you too shape the world. As your world changes and influences you, you too have the ability to change and influence your world. Your influence may not be much, but it's certainly not "nothing."

One of my favorite games is to build a sand fortress against the rising tide. I can entertain myself for hours just watching the sea slowly invade and knock it down. The ocean always wins eventually, but I'm happy just to get a chance to play the game. Life is not about victory and defeat. We all lose in the end, so you have to enjoy whatever time you get to play. Enjoy the sandcastle as it's standing. You appreciate it even more fully when you understand it'll soon be gone. The trick to life is learning to see everything in that same light.

Money, relationships, vacations, happiness and sadness: they're all fleeting and passing. They come and go. It's not depressing. It just is. It's the way things are and the lesson you should take away from this universal truth is that good times should never be taken for granted and bad times, well, they're temporary too, so buck up.

Low tide at Coast Guard Beach, Eastham.

Change will come whether you want it to or not. Like with a sandcastle getting washed away, just let go. Of course, there will always be things you want to hold on to and you should hold on to what you can, but not too tightly, because you can only hold on for so long and do so much.

Compared to an atom or even a grain of sand, I'm huge, but compared to the size of a star; I'm tiny, almost infinitesimal. I guess that leaves me somewhere in the middle. In some ways I'm big and in some ways I'm small. Likewise, in some ways I'm in control and in other ways I'm powerless. I can easily hold the sand in the palm of my hand and throw it into the sea, but it's even easier for the sea to pick me up and throw me onto the land.

I don't know how many hours I've spent digging holes and filling them back in again. Like life, it all may seem a bit pointless at times, since you don't actually accomplish anything. But I can't say that the time I spent doing it was wasted, because I had fun. I enjoyed myself. Despite what we may believe in modern society and economic theory, time is not money. That's just a Benjamin Franklin quote, which has been perverted into a modern-day slogan to spur worker productivity. Sure, we say you can "buy time" and "spend time" and "waste time," just like money, but you can't.

No amount of money can buy back youth, and the value of leisure time spent with loved ones cannot be measured in dollars and cents. To put a price tag on such things only trivializes them. We've come to associate personal productivity with personal worth. Hitler did and accomplished a lot. That doesn't make him any more important or influential than Socrates (the Greek Philosopher), who did not. Despite what your teachers and bosses and parents might say, it's ok to do nothing. Really, it is. It's ok to play in the sand, no matter how old you are. It's ok to space out and lose yourself in thought. It's even ok to "veg out" on the couch.

Being mature doesn't mean you have to stop doing what you like and what makes you feel good. Growing up means finding a balance between doing what you want and doing what you must. Mature thinking is looking at both sides of the coin and accepting the purpose and place of both ups and downs. I will get old, but I don't ever intend on growing up. What's the point? Life is not as serious as some people make it out to be.

Eventually everything you create will be destroyed. Everything you do and say will be forgotten. Even your tombstone (if you'll have one) will eventually crumble and there will be no physical evidence left that you ever even existed. Nothing you do is that important. Nothing anyone says is as important as you think it is. No mistake is unforgivable. All will be washed away. All will be erased.

So think of each day as a fresh start and a clean slate, like the sand on the beach. Enjoy whatever time you have doing whatever you're doing, because soon it will be over. Soon you'll be dead and that's ok. You're here now and even though you may not ever know it or see it, your existence has permanently changed the universe forever. How, you might ask?

Well, maybe that handful of sand you threw into the water was enough to alter the shape of the coastline over time. Or maybe that simple act of moving your hand at that moment was enough to change the rotation of a distant galaxy. It's the butterfly effect. (You know, when a butterfly flaps its wings in South America, there's a typhoon in Asia). We may be small and our existence may be short, but our mere presence will resonate far and long after we seize to exist in our present state. In this way, we all in a sense have already achieved some sort of immortality, because the only thing that doesn't change is change. We change the change, therefore because of "us" the universe will never be the same.

12 STORMY WEATHER

The forces of nature are in a constant battle and humans are but the witnesses. It is a war between gods, too great for us to take part in. Like with the waves, the only thing we can do during a storm is to ride it out. Again, it comes back to the three basic needs: food, water and shelter. Survival means securing those first because if you don't you remain like most other animals, scrounging from hand to mouth, never free to progress further or achieve greater existential goals. But no matter who you are or what you have, when the battle rages, there is little you can do but stay out of the way. Some places are safer than others, but no place is safe, especially not Cape Cod.

The Cape is precariously positioned in the path of two major weather pattern systems. It's located at the end of the Atlantic hurricane beltway and at the backhand of northern Atlantic nor'easters. I've weathered all kinds of storms and on the outer Cape the winter storms can be just as, if not more, intense than the tropical ones, which normally get weakened in the colder water.

I was on the Cape for a hurricane when I was a child. It was around Labor Day weekend and the news of it sent most of the tourists packing. For two days, both bridges were jammed with the traffic of those trying to flee the storm's path. Then the day before it hit, the roads emptied and my Dad and I remained to experience the eerie calm before the storm.

We knew the hurricane was on it's way because of the news reports but if I hadn't been looking closely because of the forecast, I probably would've never noticed any specific environmental signs of the storm's approach. Outwardly, it felt like any other normal sunny day. But underneath the obvious laid a strange anticipation. It was like you could feel it coming. The birds were acting weird, not migrating in their usual patterns. There was an energy in the air. The surf, which had been building for days, started to really pick up towards mid-day but when the sun set, the wind still wasn't much stronger than on any other windy day.

When we went to bed, it didn't seem that bad outside because the brunt of the storm didn't hit until the middle of the night. I drifted off to sleep, but it wasn't long before I was awoken by a noise. I can't remember specifically what brought me back into consciousness, but once I was up, I was up. In the darkness, the rain started to pour. The gusts of wind picked up and didn't die down. Each succeeding surge of air got stronger. The storm seemed to gather up upon itself until the winds became sustained and the gusts lashed out even more.

Laying in bed in the dark, I felt the house begin to shake. The rumble felt like an earthquake or the roar of a jet taking off. The windowpanes howled and the chimney whistled. The doors on the iron woodstove rocked back and forth and outside, I could hear debris blowing up against the side of the house and the limbs of trees snapping and crashing to the ground.

I was scared, but I wasn't terrified. There was something oddly fascinating about the shear force exploding around me. I was awe-inspired, even charmed by the storm. The fear awoke my senses and made me feel more self-consciously alive than I normally did. The suspense was exhilarating and left me bursting with energy. When the power went out, I could no longer see anything, so I shut my eyes but I could seemingly hear and feel everything that was happening around me. I could picture the house from outside and visualize the scene in real time.

I barely slept all night and arose from bed not long after sunrise. I looked outside to see a large limb down in front of the house and another one out back leaning on a broken fence. Leaves were strewn everywhere and the street out front was covered by an evenly spread layer of debris from the shredded trees and bushes.

The wind was still whipping when my Dad suggested we go see the beach. It may have sounded like a crazy idea to most people, but not to me. I was much too curious to stay at home. I wanted to see and look at the face of the storm. So we got into our van and drove toward the ocean. Some roads were completely impassible because of downed telephone poles. We had to weave around fallen branches and heavy debris scattered about. The power crews were out securing and cordoning off damaged electrical lines and most, including us, were without power.

The first beach we went to was Nauset Light. There, we didn't even try to get out of the car because the wind was too strong in the high lying, exposed parking lot. But it was there we got our first sight of the ocean. It was more furious than I'd ever seen. It looked surreal, almost static. The entire coast was a huge wash of white that extended as far out as we could see. Huge, towering waves crashed more than a mile off shore and slammed down in many successive breaks.

Winter Storm at Nauset Light Beach, North Eastham.

We circled around the parking lot and braced ourselves as we felt the wind tipping the van. From there, we didn't even attempt to go to Coast Guard Beach, which would leave us completely exposed. We drove north to Marconi Station, which offers a more sheltered parking area.

The parking lot was empty of cars, but full of sand. My dad parked the van straight into the wind with the fear it might be blown over if we parked sideways. To avoid a crosswind when exiting, we got out one at a time and met at the back of the vehicle. Sand was being hurled from the dunes and whipping across the asphalt stinging my legs in a million little places. I was so lightweight that I couldn't stand up alone. So I grabbed a hold of the back of my dad's belt and my extra weight actually served to help him out. Crouching behind him, we fought our way toward an overlook.

The boardwalk leading to the lookout was covered by sand-drifts and as we crested over the dunes, the wind blasted us. Once exposed, my father could no longer stand up, so he grabbed a fence, which led us up to the top. We didn't make it far because the wind was too strong and I couldn't see much of anything because the moving air was making my eyes water. But I caught glimpses of the storm's shear intensity. It was a sight that seemed unfit for human eyes. Mother Nature was naked in all her glory. I wanted to look. I wanted to see more. I was fascinated, captivated and mesmerized by the divinity of it. It was mind-blowing. I couldn't believe the power. You can watch a video of something like it or see a picture, but it doesn't even come close to capturing what it's like actually being there and standing among the madness.

The sea was completely untamed in its attack and the land was steadily holding its front line (although not without casualties). The choir of howling winds along with the rumble of the gigantic waves was deafening. It was like watching two giants fighting heroically. There was panic, chaos, yet somehow the whole dance seemed eerily orchestrated.

A hurricane has a life and holds a certain rhythm as it swirls northward away from the equator. The winds were warm, strangely warm for that time of year. They were winds of change balancing the atmosphere and slowly ushering in the cold winds of autumn, which sweep down to take their place. It's all a big balancing act, even the Earth, which itself seems alive by the way it constantly realigns things to maintain equilibrium.

The Earth is whirling through space, spinning back and forth, like a wobbling top. The greater universe, like the Earth and the self, is fighting its own battles with conflicting forces. War is ugly. But the sight of this natural destruction was breathtakingly beautiful. I was not only looking into the face of Mother Nature, I was looking into the face of the universal divine, the basic forces, which drive the tumult of existence. It was overwhelming from land and I can't even imagine what it would have been like at sea.

It's a pity to those who get caught in the jaws of the hungry ocean and to all living things stuck out in the storm. Your fate is in its hands and you can't do anything to change it. You can only hope it will spare you for another day. No amount of technology can stop the inevitable, not now, if ever. It's too big.

I returned to the van a different person because after you see something like that, you're never the same. You can't forget it. It's truly humbling and changes the way you think. It doesn't matter how much your ego is puffed up. It doesn't matter if you're a president or a king, the ocean does not discriminate. It'll swallow you up whole and leave no evidence of your bodily existence. You have to respect the ocean for its sheer mass. Like the subconscious, it's vast and powerful and who knows what deep dark secrets lay in its depths, which influence the world above the surface.

Back in the van, the skin on my legs was chaffed and burning. The wind was so powerful that it had sandblasted the van's windshield, which became full of tiny little dings from the sand particles being propelled into it. We left the parking lot and drove around, witnessing more of the carnage. Trees had been ripped up from their roots and one had fallen across the roof of a house. Garbage and lawn furniture was strewn everywhere through the woods near houses.

It was an amazing experience and winter storms can be just as incredible because you take all of those same elements of chaos and combine them with the element of cold, which makes it all the more severe. Imagine that same surf, but with freezing wind coming in from the north. Your chances of survival anywhere become severely diminished since hypothermia becomes an added danger. The trees gloss over with ice, causing their branches to snap under the weight. Severe nor'easter storms can eat entire stretches of beach in a single day and alter the shape of the coastline for years to come. Sandbars get shifted, channels fill-in in one place and deepen in others.

The storms don't actually create or destroy anything (besides maybe vegetation and human property). They just move things around and make changes to what's already there. They take the world one step closer to a more disorganized, yet stable state. These are the storms outside. However, storms may occur within us as well and sometimes they can seem just as powerful and transforming as those in the environment.

Personal turmoil arises during our adjustments to the ever-changing world. When something traumatic happens to us, when someone dies, when a relationship ends or when our life simply gets off track and falls out of balance, we struggle, we have a mental storm, which shifts our priorities and rearranges us into a new state of being. The old self isn't gone. It's just been re-shaped by what we have weathered (or experienced).

The world within is just as vast and violent as the world without and it can be even more difficult to find shelter from those internal storms. At times you can't and there's no avoiding the brunt of the storm. You draw the short stick or have a strike of bad luck and you're the one in the wrong place at the wrong time. Sometimes, the wheel lands on you. Houses and fences can be rebuilt, but internal wounds take much longer to heal than flesh and bones.

So like with an approaching hurricane, you have to be ready and be able to see it coming so you can anticipate it. Either get out of its way, by positioning yourself properly, or hunker down and brave it. Exposure to anything changes you. What is seen cannot be unseen. What is thought cannot be un-thought. Every event alters reality, both externally and internally. You cannot calm the outer world, but you can learn to pacify the inner one. I learned that while I was standing at the beach during a hurricane.

Even though the world around me was at war, the world within me was at peace. Having no fabricated thoughts or worries beyond my present situation, I merely observed reality without judgment or expectation. My mind was nowhere else, but on that beach at that moment and I was able to see the world for what it was: crazy and unexpected, but not completely without cause. Then and there, my self-consciousness was replaced by self-awareness and I was able to find calm during the storm.

13 CLEANING

With all of the fierce fall and winter storms, you inevitably find yourself cleaning up a lot on the Cape. The storms can do extensive damage to personal property. I was home alone once when just a typical winter storm ripped the antenna off the roof and left the mangled metal dangling off the side of the house.

Regular winter storms leave debris scattered everywhere and by the amount of broken and fallen trees, it's a wonder there are any trees still standing with all of the abuse they take. Life is a constant struggle between order and chaos. The trees, being a force of life, bring order and stability to a landscape. They anchor down the soil and hold water, factors which give the soil resistance to erosion.

I spoke about it earlier, but again, the entire universe seems to be going towards increasing disorder. We say the entropy (disorder) is increasing. That's in most places. However, there are tiny pockets in the universe, little bubbles, where the small forces seem to contradict the larger ones and the elements begin to act in defiance against the overall flow. Like swirls in a river cause some of the water to move upstream, life goes against the larger flow.

Life is not chaotic. Even a microorganism's body is highly sophisticated and organized. Organize. Organism. You can see the connection in the word. Life is the antagonist (or protagonist depending on how you look at it), which contradicts the apparent disorder of most inorganic material. Every organism, from large multi-cellular ones like humans to single celled amoebas, exhibit somewhat autonomous behavior, magically and mysteriously arising out of the otherwise unpredictable world, which doesn't seem fit to harbor such intricate complexity.

The paradox between order and chaos is rather perplexing because on the surface, life and even the fundamental laws of the universe seem so deterministic. There are basic rules that govern physical matter and under most conditions these laws are completely steadfast and unbreakable. One event leads to another and so on. In the narrowest sense, everything does happen for a reason, because it's the consequence of something else. A thousand variables lead to the inevitability of an event happening at a particular moment because the circumstances set it up in a way to happen. Theoretically, there are no exceptions and we could predict everything and logically deduce the past if we only knew and understood all of the factors involved.

Water flows downhill from the mountains to the sea because of gravity, traveling on a path of least resistance. In other words, it goes down taking the quickest and easiest path it has access to. The entire universe, including our homes, tends to flow in that same direction back toward the center, toward a more restful balanced state. It just so happens that this more stable state takes form in a chaotic fashion. Clothes don't fold themselves. You have to fold the clothes and over time they become unfolded. If a vase sitting on a table falls to the floor and shatters, it goes to a more stable and generally more disorganized state. The vase doesn't un-break and rise back up onto the table.

It takes a certain amount of energy or "work" to create that vase and put it into its organized and relatively less stable state. Life is a miracle, because it's like that vase putting itself back together. We are the rebels in this universe. The cells in our bodies conspire and work to align themselves against the tyranny of disorder. Cleaning, therefore, technically is work, because it's moving things against their natural tendencies. It's the active practice of putting things back into order, like moving the water back up hill.

When we eat, we derive energy from breaking down the chemical bonds, which have grown in the food. Whether it's meat or vegetables, we cannot eat just anything. The food we eat must have a specific order in its chemical structure to be useful to us. We feed off of the order and expel waste, which is essentially the same thing in a more chaotic, disorganized form. Other organisms have the ability to use our waste as fuel and thus the circle of life turns.

Life is a constant cycle between these "constructive" and "destructive" processes, things that create order and things that tear it apart. Therefore, cleaning is like a ritual renewal. If you leave things be, they tend to get cluttered and disorganized, so from time to time, you have to dust them off and put them back into place. The irony is that cleaning is a job that never ends. It's like bowling pins. You set things up only to be knocked down again. As soon as you clean something, it starts to get dirty. This is particularly true on Cape Cod because as I said, the harsh coastal storms thrash the forests and leave your yard and house strewn with debris.

A Weathered and Broken Seashell.

Plus, Cape Cod is made of sand and the sand tends to get everywhere. I think it's just a fact of life that no matter how careful you are, the sand somehow finds its way into your pockets and the soles of your shoes, just like dust and dirt inevitably find their way into the corners and nooks of your home and life. You can hire someone to clean up for you, but ultimately it's up to you to take care of it and get it done whichever way you choose to. However, the practice of cleaning does not only apply to your house, but to your body and your psyche as well.

From time to time, you have to clean out the cobwebs in your mind. Our brains and bodies also get cluttered and dirtied by the chaotic world around us, by stress, by negative thoughts and actions. It's even more difficult to clean out your own mental garbage than it is to clean up your house. But still, it is something that must be done and coincidentally, the outward act of cleaning can help you do it internally as well.

When you clean, you reflect on the world and move things into a certain, specific order, which serves a useful or aesthetic purpose. So cleaning can also be thought of as a Zen, meditative practice and if you treat it as such cleaning can even be a means of artistic expression. It's not "creative" in its purest sense but nothing really is. Matter and energy cannot be created or destroyed. All things arise from something else. Musicians don't create notes. They merely arrange them in a way to serve their purpose. Cleaning is part of that same creative process.

When cleaning, like when creating, there are two fundamental decisions at play. Where to put things is secondary, preceded by what to keep and what to throw away. Sometimes you need to purge, both yourself and your home, to let go of some unneeded things that link you to your past. Actively decide which items are most valuable and useful and only hold on to those that are. The question is not what we need and what we don't need, or what we want and what we don't want. The question is: Do we have space for it and does it fit into our life? Some things only serve to weigh us down.

Once you decide what stays and what goes it becomes a matter of where to put them. You can sometimes make things fit into places, which don't seem to have enough space. It's all about proper positioning. "Feng shui" generally holds the idea that where you put things affects how you behave, and how you behave affects how you think, therefore where you put things affects how you think and feel. I am no expert on feng shui and am not one to point out and proclaim strict rules. All I can say is this: you should arrange your surroundings in a way that streamlines your life and benefits your priorities. What's needed should be easily accessible and whatever space you have should be utilized to its best potential for you personally. The design must be fluid and change from time to time to fit your changing life.

Sometimes you have to switch it up. But once you find a good arrangement, you should leave things as they lay. Don't fix what's not broken, but always maintain what you have.

How organized you want your self and your life is best left up to the individual. Some people find it easier to work with a mess. Sometimes, a mess is not such a mess and “disorder” is not disorder. It only appears to be disordered to an individual, who cannot comprehend its structure or the way the system works. This makes me think about the greater world. Is it really so crazy and so chaotic as it seems or does it only seem so chaotic because we don't understand it? Maybe the order is there and we just can't see it. Maybe the two faces of Mother Nature, the caring mother and the ruthless killer, which seem to be contradictory, are not so different, but actually one in the same, since they are driven by the same energy and derived from the same forces.

Life and existence, like cleaning and things getting dirty, is a civil war, a battle within itself. We are nourished by the same forces, which eventually lead us to fall apart. Like a wave, we either release all of our energy and crash or die down after some conflicting force brings us to rest. Death and decay are nature's way of ritual cleaning. The world must get rid of the old in order to usher in and make room for the new.

Even though the world seems to be in complete disarray, it is also perfectly messed up since everything adheres to those same strict laws. The universe has a way of sorting itself out, the same way nature has a way of putting things back into place and “feng shui-ing” itself. So chaos is in many ways organized and the organization process can be seen as somewhat chaotic.

After a big storm, when the waves wash up high onto the beach and get to the dunes, the sand becomes perfectly flattened by the retreating water. Then human footsteps, over time, disrupt and disturb that natural “order.” When the waters are calm, we are the ones who are making the ripples, so as I see it, the forces driving us are indeed not so different from the ones driving the wind and the waves. We are just another part in the same system and are at times the ones, who are actually messing things up.

Looking south on Nauset Light Beach, North Eastham.

14 WALKING ON THE BEACH

Partly what makes the eastern shore of Cape Cod so majestic is that the beach seems to go on forever. It extends as far as you can see in both directions and once you start walking, you only find more and more of the same. The beach just keeps on going. The slanting embankment of sand from the water to the large dunes, the swerving lines of successive high tide marks and of course the rhythm of the waves massaging the shoreline. The beach and the waves are consistent, but in no place are they ever the same.

If you walk on the beach for long enough, you start to notice a strange order within everything. On calm days, the madness doesn't seem so mad and the waves on the water look eerily similar to the wave patterns the tide makes on the sand upon its retreat. It's the same pattern made by the wind in deserts and rivers in their beds. As the undulating water releases its energy, it shapes the contour of the shoreline into its own image.

The world tends to arrange itself in particular patterns, which the more you look the more you find in different places, both large and small. It's all from the same fundamental energy, so why wouldn't it all be shaped to fit into similar modes, which work? Let's be honest. A person is a person and a giraffe is a giraffe. Humans and giraffes might outwardly not have a whole lot in common, but if you analyze their overall structure and how they function, giraffes are not all that much different from humans. Then you look at a wave. A wave is a wave, whether it is in the water, in the air or in the sand. They might come in different sizes, lengths and heights, but again there are characteristics that unite them and make them what they are.

There's a basic design that makes a wave, like there's a design that makes a body and an airplane and a beach. An airplane needs wings and propulsion. A beach needs land and water. Probably one of nature's most fascinating designs is the bubble.

Wave Backwash at Coast Guard Beach, Eastham.

Spheres are the basic building block of life, which are created in many places, one of them being at the edge of an ocean, where the waves crash. They're perfectly balanced formations, born of turbulence and disarray.

Walking down the beach I realized that these peculiar patterns are everywhere. The energy in the wind takes shape and that shape takes a form in the design of waves, which organize and embody themselves on the surface of the water, then on the surface of the sand. It's in the grain of driftwood, in minerals in rocks and even in my own fingerprints. Look up and you'll see it in the clouds. Look down and you'll see it in the tides, the way the water ebbs and flows routinely.

This universal energy personifies itself in all mediums. The pattern is like a cycle that repeats, but never the same way. It's another one of life's contradictions. How can it even be a pattern if it doesn't repeat? The waves roll in cycles. You can predict when and where a wave is going to break by watching it. You might be able to even predict the wave behind it and the wave behind that, but you can't predict the tenth wave and a wave that's going to break two weeks from tomorrow and hasn't even formed in the water yet. The same is true for weather. We can roughly predict it three days in advance, but beyond that we're completely in the dark. You'd think it'd be easier with all of our technology.

The same goes for the tides. Yes, we have tide charts and we can accurately predict the tides for a long foreseeable future, but there is no master formula, which can predict the tides forever. You have to keep on making calculations, based on conditions, which are fluctuating as a result of other larger forces. So it's a pattern because it has a rhythm, which repeats enough to hold some degree of predictability, but at the same time lacks complete consistency and uniformity. As a result, we have a much easier time of saying what isn't going to happen as opposed to what is, and even then we are sometimes surprised about what actually takes place. Who could have predicted some of the random events that occurred both in nature and in society?

You never know what you're going to find washed up when you're walking down the beach. Mostly it'll be debris from storms or something that fell off of a shipping vessel. You might find a buoy or a dead animal and more and more often you find pieces of garbage. It's a sad truth. A dead animal might be unsightly and smell bad, but its body gets recycled and goes back into the mix. A piece of plastic just sits there and maybe it will give a small animal a home for a while, but most likely it'll lead to the untimely death of whatever eats it. Grotesque as it is, the dead animal fits in. The piece of orange plastic seems alien and out of place.

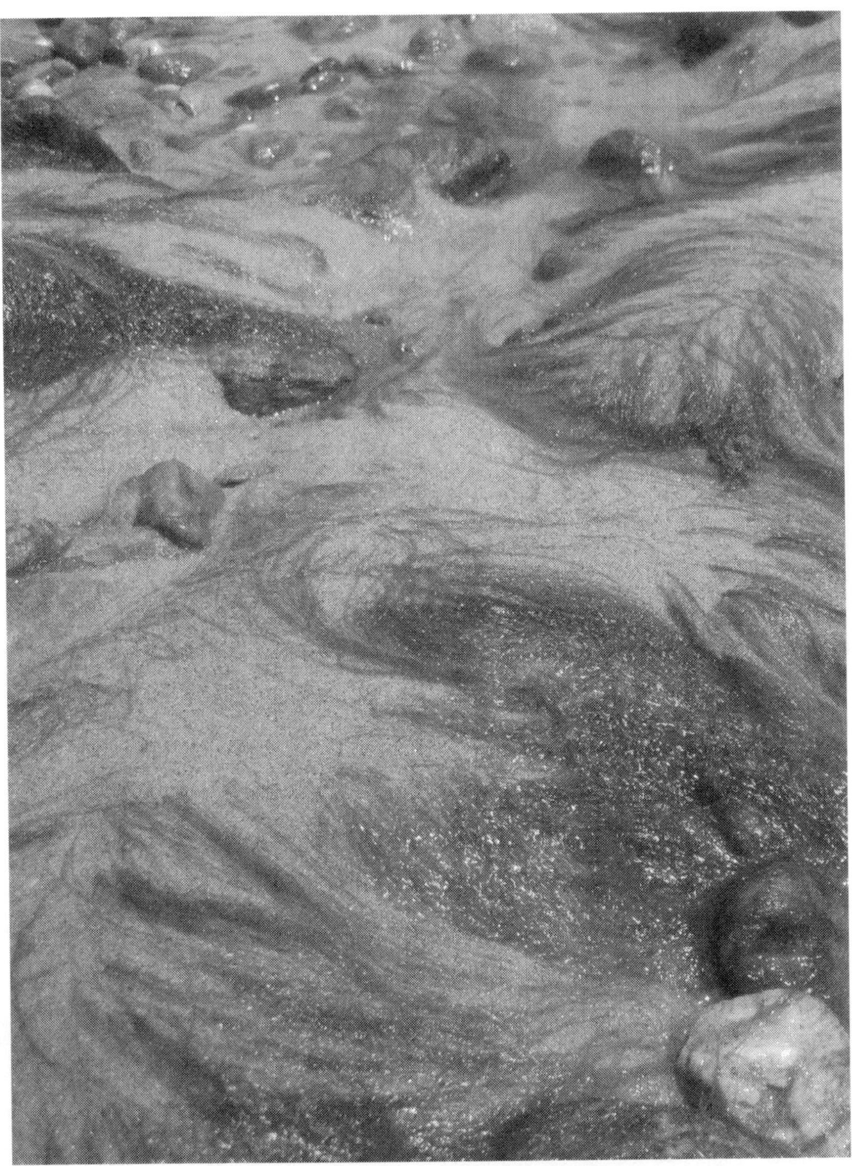

Tidal Pool at Coast Guard Beach, Eastham.

Broken Lobster Trap, Coast Guard Beach, Eastham.

I often feel out of place in society, but when I'm walking on the beach alone or with a good friend I feel like I'm in my element, like it's where I belong. The beauty of life and the universe is sometimes hard to see in the city or in the routine of modern life, but on the shore, I see the meaning of it all.

Looking ahead while walking up the beach you can't always make out what something is. You see mirages and try to fill in the gaps with your mind, but the only way to definitively figure out what lays in front of you is to keep walking and see what it is.

One day, I stumbled upon a dying seal, which had beached itself. The animal was sick and lying high up on the sand. The hours it had left were numbered and there was nothing I could do to save it. To approach it would be dangerous because it would fight back with all its might for fear I meant to harm it. There was nothing I could do to help it, but just watch it die. A day later I returned and found it dead. The animal's body lay there but its essence was gone. The electricity in its nerves had stopped firing and the life force, which had once given it animation, was no longer there.

Where had it gone, to seal heaven or seal hell? We can hypothesize and theorize all we want, but the truth is that nobody knows, because once you walk down that path, you can't ever return. Life and time, unlike the beach, are one-way streets. No matter which direction you are facing, you are always going forward and can never go back.

Sure, theoretically, if we had better sight, we would be able to see farther up the beach but we still cannot see around the bends and in truth the beach, which we are seeing up ahead of us is not the same beach that we will find when we get there. The farther ahead we look into the distance and the future, the more different it will be when we get there because with every passing second and breaking wave, the beach and the world are transforming. A new beach (and a new future) is being created at every passing moment and with every step. We cannot see what will be. We can only see what is and what has been.

Therefore, life and death and the universe are always to some extent unpredictable. The constantly changing variables make for a future of uncertainty. The beach you walked on yesterday is not the same beach you walk on today. The future of yesterday is not the future of today. Even if you do a full circle, that place which you returned to after your walk is not the same place as the place you left. Likewise, the person you are when you go to the beach is not the same as the person you are when you come back. The changes may be subtle, but they are there.

For me, one of the best parts about walking down the beach on Cape Cod is that it feels timeless. You get lost in eternity. With the dunes shielding you from development, you see the world as it is and as it has been since its creation at the end of the last ice age. You're seeing the beach the same way the first explorers did, the same way Thoreau did. It could be the year 1960, 1800 or even 500 BC and you wouldn't be able to tell the difference. It's as pure and untouched as it's been since its birth. The waves break the same way. They sound the same way. The sand feels the same way. You see the art of creation in its naked beauty, before it was tainted (or augmented) by human civilization.

Speaking of nudity, if you walk far enough away from one of the established beach entrances, you might even run into a nudist or two, people enjoying nature in their own natural form, wearing nothing but their birthday suit. That's how and when, as a teenager, I saw for the first time, firsthand, the full beauty of a naked female. My family and I accidentally stumbled upon a group of some naturalists enjoying their beach day and although most of them were old, there was a pair of young women.

One of the women stood up and walked toward the water. She cut directly in front of me and my heart skipped a beat as her naked form swayed gently. It was a boyhood fantasy come true but in retrospect I see how she fit perfectly into that place with the raw, natural beauty of the beach and the sea. The naked body, like the beach is a work of art with its flowing curves and symmetric lines. The human form is so perfectly designed that I couldn't help but stare at her, and what I saw that day was so much more than all her parts. My eyes opened in a new way. I saw her and her body and the beach and the world as a whole much greater than the sum of their parts. She was a magnificent specimen and indeed we all are. So is the world. That's when I learned not to be ashamed of my body.

Unlike the puritans, who settled much of New England and sought to cover themselves, I've come to see the body as something to be celebrated, not hidden away. Why hide something so utterly enchanting? Imagine if we covered the beach or tried to clothe animals. Why do that? It's just unnatural. I can admit that clothes hold a purpose in certain circumstances and places, but we mustn't forget that nakedness is our natural and true state. If you can't feel comfortable when naked, how will you ever feel comfortable wearing clothes? We are born naked and in many ways I believe people would be much happier if they spent more time exposed (and I don't mean just having sex).

Look at the sheer joy little kids find in stripping off their clothes and playing in the buff. They become so full of delight in their uncompromised form that we should all learn to live with such unabashed confidence as we did when we were children. How many unhealthy, self-conscious mental complexes arise from the daily ritual of clothing ourselves? We've come to think of nakedness as something out of the ordinary, something to be gawked at and seen only in highly sexualized terms. But in my opinion, this narrow view only cheapens the body and serves to degrade its real worth. I'll admit the scene with the naked women was erotic, but that's only because my eyes had never beheld such a sight.

Think about it. If everybody went to the beach naked and always had, it wouldn't be such a big deal and the image of a naked body wouldn't be so taboo. Being with my parents, I was embarrassed and for some reason felt like I had to look away. Of course, I couldn't, but just by looking at her, I felt as if I was doing something wrong. How messed up is that? How messed up has society made us? My desire to look at her wasn't out of deranged perversion but out of natural curiosity. It's so unfortunate that our uptight morality frowns upon the image of a naked human body and it makes me think, what other naked truths does society try to hide from us?

No matter how differently we act humans are just animals in many ways. We can pretend all we want, cloud our brains with moral standards, logic and religious mumbo jumbo. But at the end of the day, the evidence stacks up against us. We have to eat and sleep, just like animals. Our anatomy is almost exactly the same as all other mammals and even our bodily functions and processes work no differently than other beasts. Our clothes and our pompous, righteous behavior try to hide and disguise the simple truth that underneath it all we are mortal, naked animals. We can learn to control our impulses, but we can never eliminate them completely.

Like the beach, we shouldn't disrespect our bodies or trash them. It's possible to enjoy them both, without permanently defacing them. Bodies, like the beach, shouldn't be bought and sold. In fact, they can't really be owned. We might inhabit the materials of our flesh for a time, but ultimately nothing in this world can be possessed.

There are places on Cape Cod where you can own the beach, but who has the right to grant someone the authority to own anything, especially the Earth. If it goes by first come, first served, then all of the land and beaches on Cape Cod were stolen from the natives and the animals, which inhabited them before us. We may write deeds, but in truth we have no right to claim them. All things, even our bodies are on loan. We can do what we want with them while we have them, but in the end, all will be returned.

How many problems could be solved and how many wars could be stopped if people didn't think and act so possessively? We can draw a line in the sand and say you shall not pass, but these lines do not exist physically. They are only in our heads. The man-made boundaries and arbitrary markers we project onto the world only serve to box us in. The real world is united and boundless.

On the beach and in life, there is no “yours” and “mine.” The natives knew these basic truths, which we no longer seem to value and respect in this winner-take-all, take as much as you can grab mentality. In the real world, there are no limits. Where the land ends, the ocean begins. It's so obvious when you're standing at the edge of the sea. That's why a simple walk on the beach can be more enlightening than reading existential philosophy. With the sand between your toes, it's easy to let your mind be free. Maybe those nudists are on to something. Free your body to free your mind. Or is it free your mind to free your body? Either way, the more you reveal and the less you hold onto, the more liberated you'll feel.

15 PROVINCETOWN

Provincetown sits on the outer-most tip of the curling Cape and of the numerous fishing villages is by far the most unique, both for its character and its location. For all practical purposes, it's like the end of the Earth. Once you get there, the roads simply dead end and most likely because of its distance and seclusion Provincetown has become a rendezvous point for people, who don't always seem to fit into the rigid confines of mainstream society.

I'll be the first to admit that Cape Cod in general is not a melting pot of diversity. In other words, most people who live on or frequent the Cape tend to be white and from a similar socio-economic background. That's not to say that Cape Cod doesn't hold diversity and poverty. It does, but let's just say that Provincetown adds a whole rainbow of color because it's a place where you're more likely to see two men holding hands than a man and a woman.

In the summer, there are parades of drag queens and schools of well-groomed people filling the streets. Straight people become the minority and it's been like that for as long as I can personally remember.

Going to Provincetown as a child, I never thought much of seeing two women holding hands or two men kissing. The truth is, in my innocence, I didn't care. What did it matter if two men liked to kiss? Kissing is kissing. It isn't fighting. The atmosphere was so light and jovial that it felt like a carnival and I just thought that that's how the people were in Provincetown. I always loved going there because it was unique and interesting, both socially and geographically.

It wasn't until I got a little older that I was informed that those people in Provincetown were, gasp, different. They were called "gays" and "queers" and many other ugly words. It's crazy because the people I saw in Provincetown looked no different from the "normal" people I saw everyplace else. Then I learned that those people didn't just live in Provincetown. They lived everyplace but most times where they lived forced them to hide who they were and who they wanted to kiss. Only there, in Provincetown, could they openly act as they wanted, because what's fair game in P-town is generally unacceptable on the streets of many other cities. I like that and I think it's good for everybody, not just homosexuals. What is sexual preference anyway? Simply a taste.

I happen to be attracted to a certain type of woman and many guys like girls that I could never find attractive. The point is that these are all just personal preferences. I don't like cheesecake. No joke. I don't. Some people love cheesecake. They're crazy about it and ask me "How can you not like cheesecake?" and I say, "I don't know. I just don't." So you know what? I don't eat it. I can respect the fact that other people like it and I'm certainly not going to tell somebody else they can't or shouldn't eat it because I don't like it. People are people. Love is love. Kindness is kindness. What difference does it make what parts of a person you are drawn to or with whom you want to share your kindness?

The life-lesson that Provincetown has taught me is that you don't have to do something the way others or the majority do it. Sometimes the majority is wrong. Look at slavery, segregation and Jim Crow laws. People are not perfect and neither are any of the institutions they've ever created. Laws do not always align with what's right and ethically correct. Some people like cats. Others like dogs and many like both. I might not be attracted to other men, but I can respect the fact that other men are and as long as their behavior is not impeding or imposing upon mine, I personally don't care what they do in their private lives. It's not my business.

Sometimes, I wonder what it would be like if the whole world was like Provincetown and to be a straight man living in a gay man's world? I'd hope they wouldn't force me to do things I didn't want to do or criminalize my behavior just because of my taste.

Conformity is fickle because sometimes it is needed to create social order. Take driving on the right side of the road for example. It's absolutely necessary for the benefit of all. If everybody drove however they wanted, the streets would be chaos and nobody would ever get anywhere because they'd be blocking each other from every direction. Therefore we willingly and happily sacrifice a piece of personal freedom for our own benefit. Conformity in this case is useful because one's actions directly impact the actions of others in a public setting. But I can't say that it's right or necessary to dictate the lives of people when they're not in public and their actions don't directly affect the lives of others. All of the worst governments and institutions in history have tried it: Hitler and the Nazis. Stalin and the Communists. Even the Pope and the Catholics did it during the Spanish Inquisition. Strict social conformity is the bane of advanced civilization.

Personally, I too have been a victim of these social norms. When I was little, I loved playing piano. I begged my parents to get me lessons and they did. I started learning music, but as I got older, the social attitudes of my small town sucked me in. I became consumed by sports and gossip and stopped playing in the school band because I was led to believe it wasn't cool or worthwhile. I was class president, captain of the soccer team and aspiring to go to an Ivy League college. I did community service, got straight A's and jumped through all of the hoops society demanded of me, but none of it brought me happiness because I wasn't being true to myself. I did, not what I liked to do, but what I was supposed to do and it nearly drove me insane.

That's when I ran away to Cape Cod and realized the truth. Life and youth are short and any time spent being insincere is time wasted. I thought about the vacationers in Provincetown and how much joy they found when they could be out in the open and relented how they must have felt back in the "real" world. They shouldn't have to live that way and neither should I.

Provincetown Pier.

Of course, my petty plights were nothing compared to their real oppression, but it made me understand how all people are put under pressure to be and act in a certain way and how that negativity reproduces itself and gets passed on. If you really want to change the world or have any sort of meaningful existence, you must first find the courage to accept yourself and change your own behavior.

I'm thankful that my parents took me to Provincetown at a young age so I was able to witness such an open atmosphere before being tainted by social bias and judgment. It taught me a valuable lesson because before I thought of them as "gay," I thought of them as happy (which not so coincidentally just so happens to be another definition for the word). What I will always remember is not sexual deviance or moral perversion, but people laughing, smiling and being nice to one another. How fitting it was to spend every Independence Day in a place where people can truly be free. We went there for the fireworks, but I often think the founding fathers and mothers would be proud to know they set the foundation and gave the potential for such a place to exist.

That's how Provincetown and the Cape taught me that being different is ok. You are who you are, so be yourself. Do what you like and like what you do. As long as it's not hurting anyone else or imposing upon their will, it's ok, regardless of what closed-minded people might say. Be proud of who and what you are. It's a miracle just to be alive.

16 THE MOVIES

It's always nice to see a matinee on a rainy day, especially when it's a good film. You can just as easily watch a flick at home, but there's something special about experiencing a movie on the big screen in the company of others, laughing and crying together.

Nowadays, movies have become the highest form of art, combining music, dance, art and literature. Motion pictures take on an autonomous life and give you a glimpse into another world. They induce the senses and manipulate the mind. So long as people are willing to suspend their disbelief and buy into the picture, the movie becomes real in the minds of its audience. Some movies accurately depict the world we live in while others show us a world, which isn't or one that could be.

Like a walk on the beach, a movie helps to temporarily relieve your mind by removing your concentration from everyday life. A good movie not only captivates and entertains, it transforms the viewer in some way, whether it satisfies or not. Sometimes it's good to be pleased, other times it's best to be left wanting more. Either way, a great movie enlightens and changes one's perspective.

Movies may not be real, but the feelings and attitudes they create no doubt are, because movies are art and art is power, which can be used as both a tool and a weapon. The best art is neither. Great art is simply a light shining into the darkness. It reveals things we might have otherwise missed. Movies take big ideas and put them into small packages, distilling the information into tiny doses. They are a microcosm of life, and like a life, every movie starts at one point and ends at another, traveling from point "a" to point "b" in between.

Drive-in movie theatres are a different story, especially when you're young because they're not actually a place you go to watch movies. For young lovers, drive-ins are a dating ritual and serve as a non-threatening venue for teenagers to mingle. Why go to the drive-ins? It's partially because there're not many other places for teens to go out but also because there are few other settings parents will let you be alone in the dark with a member of the opposite sex.

Sometimes just the act of being in close proximity brings two people closer together. Humans in general are gregarious. They want to be close to each other and in fact, one should never lose touch with that frisky teenager, which once ruled you. Of course it's necessary to mature, but you should try hard to hold onto the piece of yourself, which once saw the world with wonder. Simple curiosity not only propels exploration and discovery, but it's also a great remedy for boredom and breaking the monotony many adults fall into.

Even as you age it can still be fun to go to the drive-in and act like those teenagers again, to just sit next to each other and do the little things, like holding hands and making out. It's what drive-in movies beg of you. The set up is perfect and in many ways what they were made for.

I remember being in the back of my Dad's SUV with a friend and two girls we had met on the beach. Nothing happened sexually, but we drank and smoked and did all of the things kids at that age aren't supposed to do. It was awkward, innocent and pure. We laughed and had fun, but didn't do anything dangerous or stupid. Come to think of it, in many ways, I acted much more responsibly back then when I was a teen than I did when I was in my twenties.

While aging, our lives somehow grow so much more complex and complicated. They become even more unpredictable than even the craziest movies. After all, real life is so much grander than what can be captured on screen for two to three hours time. The most comic and compelling story of all is the one that is being experienced by you. It's happening every day all around you. Your life is the greatest story ever told and the most epic saga.

No love story can simulate the feeling of actually being in love because it's a fundamentally different practice to do something than it is to watch something. There is no comparison to watching kissing and to actually kiss. So although movies may be able to induce a sense of emotion and impact your memories, they don't compare to raw, uncensored life. Movies are highly edited and directors go to great lengths to make sure we see only what they want us to see. Real life is uncut and contains much more detail than any movie can capture. Sure, real life doesn't always flow like a good movie, but no doubt there will be twists and turns along the way.

Sometimes life is all too real. There is too much information and too many side plots, so it can be hard to follow since there are no subtitles or narrator to clarify what's happening. On the flipside, life can also get unimaginably dull and boring, so a good movie now and then can help break the monotony and take you out of it for a while. If you get preoccupied while watching a movie, it's no big deal. You can always rent it, press pause and rewind to watch it again. However, in life there are no second viewings, so you'd better pay attention and keep looking, otherwise you might end up missing the point completely.

17 BY NIGHT

The nights of Cape Cod seem to be especially dark because in many places there are no streetlights and the beach (in some areas) has little light pollution. On cool nights, when the sky is clear and the moon isn't out, the stars shine brilliantly. There seem to be millions you can see and who knows how many millions you can't.

One night, while I was visiting the beach alone, an interesting thing happened to me. I was staring up at the stars for a long time and after a while they seemed to look three-dimensional. Maybe it was just my eyes playing a trick on me, but it seemed as though the brighter stars were closer and popping out of the black background, while the dimmer stars sat back further away on the canvass. I could imagine the band of stars forming a long arm extending out from the Milky Way galaxy and at that moment my entire perspective on life changed. I suddenly felt like I was no longer looking up, but rather looking out. I was not on top of the world, but rather peering off the side of it. I could see the bigger picture and maybe it was only an illusion, a mental image, but then again isn't everything?

Many of the stars we gaze at are already dead so what we see is not actually there. We're looking at the light from a past existence, so in a way when we look out into space we aren't looking out into an infinite abyss, we're actually looking back in time on a universe which used to be. If we could somehow travel faster than the speed of light and get to the locations of those stars at that same point in time, we'd find nothing there except the remnants of their past glory. But how can that be? How can something simultaneously exist and not exist at the same time? Well, it all depends on where you are.

Time is kind of like a wave. The farther out to sea you are, the earlier you make contact with that wave (event). A fisherman feels a wave long before it crashes onto the beach. As I've already stated, the wave (and everything in the entire universe) is merely a flow of energy moving from one point, its creation to another, its degradation. Imagine that these universal waves only crash when they encounter a black hole, but others just keep going out forever. Time is essentially the measurement of these passing waves and of the overall evolving universe.

In reality there are no definite points in time because everything is moving in one direction, toward progression. What we perceive as definite points, like the sunrise and sunset are merely rhythmic coincidences, which result from our place and perception. Days, months and years only exist in relation to where we are because the sunset and sunrise are happening constantly and simultaneously, just changing place in the world with every passing moment. What one perceives as sunrise, another sees as sunset. That's relativity or the idea that time (and space) is subject (or relative) to perspective and point of view. Theoretically, time travel is possible if we could just build a boat that went faster than the wave (or in universal terms the speed of light).

Humans use certain cyclical events to measure time, but in the grand scheme of things, those markers are just arbitrary points on a multidimensional graph of changing variables. Time passes seamlessly and everything, from large to small, is constantly shifting. No particle of matter in the universe is ever stationary. The Earth and all of the stars are actually wandering through "space" and expanding in size. We just don't notice it all of the time because everything is doing it at a constant rate and almost perfectly proportionally to everything else.

Waves (and time) may shift course and get interrupted, but once they break, they don't seem to un-break. With each passing moment, the world is evolving into something brand new and although things may appear to be pretty much the same from moment to moment, in all actuality everything has changed. Nothing like "now" has ever existed before and chances are slim that it will ever happen again in the near future. Deep down, I think all people know this somewhat instinctually. We may not always consciously see it, but we subconsciously sense it and we humans, as living organisms, don't like it because we are attached to our selves and our lives. Biologically, we crave stability, yet our universe provides us nothing but change. Even with modern science and technology we're still missing a lot of pieces in the puzzle.

There's so much more we don't know than what we do know. Maybe our perception and beliefs are being tricked so everything we think and see is wrong. Perhaps just one missing piece might once again completely change the way we look at things. After all, appearances can be deceiving. It appears as if the sun and the stars are spinning around us, and for thousands of years, people believed they did. It seemed so obvious, until a few clever humans realized it is we who move and not the sun. Perhaps there are even grander illusions, which are making us view our reality in an equally skewed way.

Standing on the beach and looking up at the stars, I feel like I can see the grand scheme of things, that I'm stuck to the side of a giant spinning ball and whipping through space around a massive orb emitting electromagnetic energy. Just like Cape Cod's unlikely existence at the edge of the mighty ocean, the Earth sits uneasily balanced amidst a vast ocean of perceived nothingness. It seems to be an unlikely miracle that life and our precious Earth can survive amidst such harrowing circumstances and that somehow within all of this chaos, tiny bubbles can reproduce themselves into bigger bubbles and inside those bubbles, for a brief time, there is peace.

Scanning the night sky, it all feels suspiciously like a bubble, with the horizon circling around and the dome of stars bending up overhead still I wonder. How did such an unforgiving, hectic universe manage to spawn such intricate and delicate creatures such as us? Is it really a miracle or rather the result of inevitability? When you have infinite time and endless space with constant change, there is no limit to the possibilities.

I'm sure the bubble we live in will pop someday. It's only a matter of time. But for now, we are here and can live happily inside it, even if it's just an illusion. Whether or not the universe is actually real, it doesn't really matter because our perception of it makes it real, so like a dream, during the time we are experiencing it, it is real.

The apparent chaos can seem confusing, mind-blowing really and I don't think you will ever find peace if you look for it outwardly. Peace and comfort can only come from within. We are not just like the bubbles. We are the bubbles. Or I should say that we are an organized alliance of billions of bubbles. The complexity of the universe is inconceivable, almost as inconceivable as our body and our brain. Existence in itself makes you perfect, just like the universe. I can't even begin to see how it happened and I seriously doubt we'll ever be able to crack the code to life's biggest mysteries, but the why? Why do we exist? For me, that's easy. There's only one reason: to experience, because the universe itself is nothing without something (like us) to perceive it. Our perception confirms the universe's existence and therefore our purpose is merely to bear witness to it.

Even if we may not be able to control much of anything, our presence by itself is of utmost importance to everything that "is." We validate existence. We make it real. So in a way, the universe can't exist without us, the same way we can't exist without it. We are that important, not just as individuals, but as life-forms. After looking up at the stars for many nights, I've come to believe that maybe life itself is a force, just like gravity or magnetism, because life will exist anywhere it can and the ocean is a testament to that with its rich diversity and staggering array of mutated species. If you want to see the magical splendor of creation, then look no farther than the water's edge on Cape Cod at night, when it's sometimes aglow with life, literally.

With the lighthouse spinning around and shining ripples across the water, I turn away from the stars, bend down and scoop up some of the cool sand in my hand. In an instant, the sand sparkles with tiny bluish green lights. Then I look up to see a wave crashing and in the churning whitewater glisten phosphorescent algae making their own light, like little stars in the ocean. The light of life and creation burns in all living things. We are not just a reflection, like the moon. We are burning hot like the sun. We are the strange pattern, which contradicts the apparent chaos and we might not be able to find all of the answers, but at least we can ask the questions and that in itself is enough.

18 WINTER OF DISCONTENT

Winter on Cape Cod can be testing. I've been there many times and it gets weird. The coldness and seclusion gets into your head and can be downright depressing. Many of the stores and restaurants close down after the summer crowds thin out and although it's nice to be there without the traffic and confusion, seeing all of those places empty and boarded up makes you feel kind of like you're living in a ghost town. The population doesn't support the infrastructure. There's too much space, physically and socially.

I spent the good part of one winter basically alone on the Cape and in some ways I'd recommend doing it, especially if you want to learn more about yourself. But I must warn, if you really find yourself, you're not always going to like what you see. I think if I'd had a partner then it wouldn't have been so bad, but the longer I stayed there alone, the more I got lost.

Up until mid-November, I was ok and managing. The fall storms were kicking up good swells and the temperature of the water was still relatively warm, so I could go surfing often. But as the days got shorter, I started to play with fire. I'd go surfing alone, a big mistake, which I realized clearly one day while I was out by myself in the fog.

I couldn't see where the waves were breaking. But I could hear the sound of their crashing, so I paddled out beyond them and sat in silence. When a big set came, I watched the first wave come crashing through the mist and it crushed me. I resurfaced completely unaware of which way the beach was and was immediately reminded by the next wave, which came barreling in. I couldn't see the shore, but I trusted the waves to bring me there.

Landing on the beach, I was shaken and trembling with adrenaline coursing through my veins. But still I went back the next day when it wasn't foggy. The waves were even bigger and it freaked me out again being alone. But in some sick and twisted way, I liked the fear. It comforted me. It was like a bad romantic relationship, which I couldn't stay away from. I felt like I needed it, because it distracted me from my own physical and mental desolation.

That autumn I let everything go, until my life was empty and that emptiness nearly bored me to death. I longed for passion and connection. I yearned for life's lust. Trapped inside my own head, I learned to love danger because only when I was in a life-threatening situation (or inebriated) did I feel all right. It didn't matter what I thought, believed or wanted anymore. The loneliness stung my consciousness and the isolation began to eat away at me. Drowning in seclusion, my head dipped below the surface.

The madness initially came in the form of exhilaration. I became filled with an inflated zest for adventure and sometimes a social bubbly-ness. At public events I was the life of the party and conductor of the crazy train. But my moods quickly burned out and halfway through the night I became a blubbering mess. I would wake up at dawn in the middle of the woods with fuzzy recollections of how I got there and wearing only one shoe. I was never able to find the other one.

The cracks in my character started to show. My once slow and steady decline picked up as I proceeded further and further down the slippery slope. I started to compromise my own integrity and do things I wouldn't normally do even when I was of sound mind. As the weather grew colder, so did I. I forgot the obvious truths and became obsessed with my own selfish thoughts. I felt like a failure and in so many ways I was one, so I started to wonder what it was all about.

"What's the point?" I thought alone out loud. It's a dangerous question to ask yourself when you've built such high mental walls. I tried to be my own psychiatrist and self-medicate. It was red wine, at first, then whiskey on the rocks. Not before long I had to increase my dosage and for a while I was able to pretend I was ok and in control, but I was anything but. One day, I found myself drunk before the sun had set and knew consciously it wasn't a good thing. But I couldn't help it and that feeling only made me feel worse. I tried not to care, but it's so difficult not to.

Eventually my once crazy mood swings stopped and I was flat, always the same, always down. To compensate, I acted even crazier. I'd get wasted as soon as I woke up and do things you should never do when you're drunk, like going out fishing on someone else's motorboat at two o'clock in the morning. Sure, we knew the coastline and had driven the path a million times, but there's no justification. We're lucky we didn't end up dead.

I stopped sleeping and even drinking didn't help. I was depressed and I knew it. But I wanted to keep going. I wanted to go deeper, down the rabbit hole, just to see how deep it went. You can only imagine.

On my friend's birthday, we went out to a bar and chatted with some girls. After a few drinks I mocked them to their faces and could see they were in love with my friend but despised me. I knew I was an ass and the worst part was I didn't even care. I held little regard for others and even less for myself. I was free, like a bird, or so I thought. Riding home that night I had to stick my head out of the window to keep myself from throwing up. My friend thought it was hilarious and so did I.

When I made it back to the house, I once again ran off into the woods. That's the last thing I remember until just before sunrise the next morning when I woke up in the forest lying in a pile of my own vomit. I saw the warning lights flashing before me and knew I had gone too far. I tried to lighten up, but the mind is such a crazy place to get lost in. It's like a maze and once you start to open doors, you realize some were better off left shut.

There are some pretty weird things hidden in the basement of your subconscious and trust me, they're not really safe exploring without some sort of professional assistance. You're safer above ground, where their influence can be kept to a minimum. It's a complete freak show down there, like the bottom of the ocean, where monstrous looking creatures roam without light. Everything becomes scary in the dark.

Winter progressed and the world only grew fainter. All of the colors blurred into a shade of grey, melancholy. I fell into a routine, which helped, but only as much as gauze helps a bullet wound. Too stuck in my bad habits to change, I found myself talking to myself. It started off as thinking out loud, just to use my voice. Then the conversations and arguments became more complex. I fought with myself.

At the time I was finishing my first novel and became completely obsessed with it. I worked ten-plus hours a day, alone, editing, trying to make something great, but in the end I knew it was not, so after all my hard work, I didn't feel proud. I was left with the notion I had wasted all that time. I hated it. I wanted to delete it from my computer and destroy all the copies I had printed.□ I had done so much in my life, but at that point I was going nowhere.

After my first failed attempt, I started a second book and got to the point where all I wanted to do was be alone and write and play music. I was so selfish. I didn't want anybody else to hear or read it. I no longer even wanted to see my friends because they were the only thing that was helping me to hold onto the shred of sanity I still had left.

Desperately wanting to let go and give up, I ran from every opportunity. I no longer went to parties. There was no more surfing or fishing or kayaking. I stayed inside all day and stopped going to the beach altogether, except for the few times I might wander there to empty my tears into the sea. When my tears ran dry, I dug down deeper to hide. I stopped eating because I stopped being hungry and consumed just enough to keep my body functioning. Already thin, I lost weight and became skin and bones. But still, I drank and drank, but the thirst never went away, so I went on drinking, even if I didn't get drunk anymore. My tolerance grew and with no longer any escape from reality, I was forced to face my problems head on.

I felt forsaken by the Cape. She had lured me there with hopeful opportunity, beauty and charm, then left me sleeping every night alone. Truthfully, I didn't mind waking up in an empty house because there was nobody else there to bother me. The only problem was I bothered myself more than anything. I reached a state of catharsis with no compass or reference to where I was. I stopped trying to hold on and completely lost my mental bearings. It was like I was floating through an infinite sea of nothing. Without gravity, there was no up or down.

Somehow I got lost in the place I had grown up. Everything looked so familiar, but something had changed. It was I. The waves broke the same way they always had but they no longer spoke to me. Maybe I didn't understand them anymore or maybe I just stopped listening. When I seized to appreciate life in general, I fell out of love with it. That's how I came to realize that without constant care and attention everything quickly falls apart: relationships, cars, houses, etc. It's simply neglect.

If you don't tend the garden it will not flourish. If you stop tending the self, it too will no longer bear fruit. "But who cares?" I thought. All flowers wither and die with time anyway, so what's the point in even growing them to begin with. All water eventually moves to the sea. All life ends in death. Whether it's sooner or later, it doesn't matter that much. I contemplated death and concluded it wasn't so bad after all. When I started thinking like that, I knew I needed to do something.

I did an online psychological analysis and it concluded that I was exhibiting many of the symptoms of clinical depression. I knew if I told anybody what I was thinking, it would confirm their suspicions, but I thought maybe it was time I did. So to try and break my funk, I decided to throw a party.

I invited all of my old friends to come in from out of town and visit me for a winter bash. I planned it weeks in advance and was really looking forward to it. That was until a huge snowstorm blew in and nobody could make it. I ended up sitting in the house alone that day pondering, "maybe it's better off this way." If they had come, I probably would have only got crazy drunk and made an ass out of myself. Perhaps it was for the best they didn't see me in that state.

Of course, I didn't really believe it. I felt doomed and alone. That's the worst place you can be. We're all doomed in the end, but luckily we don't have to live alone. I needed out. I needed to escape from the Cape, the same place I had run away to for freedom nearly ten years before.

Pushed to the limit, I realized what I already knew. You can't live a healthy life at any extreme. Balance is everything. If you want to surf or bike or love, you have to be able to find some level of stability in yourself. I was in danger, about to cross lines I couldn't go back from and break in ways that might not be able to be fixed. So in the middle of a snowstorm, I left the Cape and sought out family.

I went to live with my brother in the mountains for a while, a long way away from the ocean and realized that everyplace, no matter how beautiful or how ugly has the ability to be heaven or hell. It's all what you make of it. That's how Cape Cod taught me the most important lesson of all: that it matters not where you are but whom you're with. No matter how special a place may be, it's no substitute for good people. Good food may nourish the body, but only good company can nourish the soul.

19 SUNRISE TO SUNSET

Although I might warn any faint of heart tourists about spending an entire year on the Cape, I highly recommend that everyone spend a complete day at the beach, sunrise to sunset. A day like that brings a life in itself and leaves you feeling tired physically, but mentally refreshed. I've done it many times, mostly by accident, as a result of all night partying and the urge to go surfing at dawn.

In the early hours of the morning, the beach is empty, save maybe for a lonely fisherman or a jogger running at dawn. If you haven't slept at all, it's truly a surreal feeling to be sitting out there on a surfboard in utter delirium as the sun slowly peaks above the horizon. With the mist rising off of the water and weak muscles, it feels like a hazy dream with the swells rocking you back and forth and the heat of the morning sun warming you like a blanket.

After sunrise surfing, I'd go to the beach and sleep a pseudo-slumber in the sand listening to the sloshing of the waves. When the sun got higher in the sky, I'd use my board to give me shade until the heat was too hot to bear anymore and I'd wake up to go surfing again for a few more hours.

By mid-morning, the beach was packed with all of the people, who were just at their start. I, on the other hand, would eat some lunch and take another nap, while the sun ever so slowly crept higher in the sky overhead.

The heat of the day is by far the most uncomfortable part, especially if you've been there since dawn. By that point, your skin starts to get burned and your body fights to stay hydrated. The sun becomes the bane of your existence and you curse it for casting no shadows anywhere to hide under. The sand is hot and the beach starts to feel like an oven, which is cooking you. At that point, the cold water becomes your only relief, until later in the day when you're able to catch some shade from the dunes or your board again.

The late afternoon and early evening is when, for me, the magic really starts to happen. The atmosphere relaxes and the tints of every color deepen into richer, warmer hues. Like a fine wine, which takes age to bring out its full flavor, a day in its mature stage offers subtle nuances that a morning (or a young wine) lack. The air stays warm, but the sun, as the angle of its rays decrease, releases you from the grip of its intense heat. Then the character of the beach completely transforms.

The mid-day bathers pack up, head off and the population on the beach thins out, leaving only the stragglers, who got there late and the ones, like me, who can't find any reason to leave. The remaining visitors automatically spread themselves out, dispersing evenly the way particles spread naturally in air to equally occupy the empty space. They organize themselves into patterns like crystalline structures. In fact, our entire society forms a macrocosm, a greater whole, the same way individual cells form a larger body. Humans consume matter like fire. Each of our bodies is a little flame and like a storm, we are composed of water, wind and electricity. It's what a day at the beach can help you to understand. When you slow down and allow your mind to wander, you get to thinking about some pretty fantastic things and thinking is probably the most important thing you can do to help yourself.

Although it seems rather elementary, there are too many times in modern life when we stop thinking. We get into a routine and go on autopilot. We habitually do what we normally do and rely on previous behaviors to dictate our future actions. Once our minds get consumed by everyday life, we stop acting consciously. Sure, as long as we are alive, our brain is functioning to keep us breathing and our heart is pumping, but contemplation is an active mental activity, which takes focus. The beach has always given me that focus and the opportunity to explore those places in my mind, which I am normally too busy to even bother acknowledging.

It's healthy for your mind to get lost in your thoughts because if you listen long enough, the world starts to tell you things. If you look around, you start to notice the tiny things, which are just as important as the grand. Each passing wave, big or small, plays its part in this cosmic play we are living. There are many forces and motivating factors, which drive the plot like characters in a story.

We can only see so much and our vision is not only limited by the frailty of our senses, it's censored by our conscious minds. Our brains filter the world and feed us a chewed up, half digested version of reality. So in everyday life, we don't simply stop noticing things we find unimportant, we stop seeing them altogether because our brain organizes and prioritizes the information it receives. It takes focus to see those little things we've stopped paying attention to. If we let it, our brain will feed us whatever distorted reality we want to see. It's important to actually look and not just see, to actually listen and not just hear.

There's nothing like lucid dreaming on the beach and letting your mind slip in and out of whatever reality you happen to be stuck in. Sometimes, while I'm dozing, I imagine things happening, only to wake up and find them not as I dreamed. I dream of being in other places at other times but when I wake up back on the beach, I always think, "perfect."

At sunset, I go surfing one last time and watch the shadows fall across the land and sea. When the wind of the day dies down, the swells roll in on a glassy surface, which reflects the radiating colors from the sky above. Slowly, the glowing orb, which lights our world falls below the perceived edge of the Earth and even after it's gone, a wonderful radiance remains that floods the world with divine illumination.

After a day like that, I go to bed knowing I truly lived and if you know you've made the most of your day, you're never sad to see it end. I guess you could say the same about life. Lying in bed, I don't think. My bones and muscles, sore from a long day of exertion finally relax. I take a couple of breaths and I'm gone.

Sunset at Briarwood Marine Science Center, Bourne.

20 FINAL REFLECTIONS

To me, heaven is Nauset Light Beach on a warm summer's evening, with a gentle swell rolling in at mid-tide. I can just think about it and I'm there. To me, Cape Cod is not just a place. It's a part of me and I take it with me wherever I go. I can still feel the ocean and the beach no matter how far away I might be.

If there's one thing I've learned throughout all of my adventures on Cape Cod it is to always "be where you are." So if you're in a place you like, recognize it and enjoy it. If you're not, do whatever you must to get out of there and put yourself in a position where you are. Sometimes that means running away. Other times that means staying. No matter where you are and what you are doing, live it.

We're always on the path toward balance, but we never actually get there (except perhaps in death). Life is a constant struggle and we may sometimes, by coincidence, find fleeting moments of peace along the way. But those moments are only temporary and short-lived, like a wave as it is breaking. The world isn't merely changing. It is transforming with each passing second and we are doing the same. We are not just like the universe, we are the universe, being an extension of it. After all, we literally are made up of star stuff.

The Native Americans were animists. They believed that everything had a spirit; the rocks and trees, the land and sea. I have to agree with them in some sense. Even according to modern science, everything that exists has mass and all mass is a form of energy. You can call the energy whatever you like, but its name is unimportant.

Different cultures all have their own words for "wave" and "sun" and "sky," but these entities are not defined by their name. They are what they are because of what they do, no matter what you call them. Even if inanimate objects, like rocks, might not be alive in a biological sense, they do contain a force within them and that force is not such a far stretch from the idea of a spirit. It's just different language used to express a similar idea.

The Native Americans hundreds and thousands of years ago saw and experienced the world just as our eyes see it today. Even with all of our technological advances, we still remain just as in the dark and perplexed about the fundamental questions of our nature and existence. We are still fighting the same demons and trying to find reason and order in events, which seem to happen chaotically.

Why do the storms blow? We can say it's the result of a pressure gradient, which causes moisture to be sucked up from the surface and eventually precipitate back down to Earth. However, that merely describes the how, not the why. Truth is, I'm not sure why the wind blows and why the rain falls. I'm not sure why a lot of things are the way they are. But in the end, I don't think it really matters. I've come to believe that the question is more important than the answer and deep down in our gut we all know what's really important in some way or another. Our minds simply get so clouded by auxiliary and artificial noise that we no longer listen to the ultimate truths, which speak quietly to us.

The Cape lets you behold those basic truths of life first hand and teaches the most important lesson of all: the simple concept of "now." Don't ever neglect the present. Don't take it for granted because it is all there ever is. Now is the only thing for sure that actually exists. The past is only expressed in the present and the future only exists in its potential. "Now" is what joins the two and separates what is and what isn't. It is the point (0,0) on a Cartesian plane, the center of everything. At this location it all comes together and connects it.

What is the "it" we always speak of? I don't know. The same "it" we speak of when we say, "it rains" or "it snows." You can call it God or the universe or whatever, but again the words are not important, their meaning is.

Modern life can be pretty overwhelming and it's easy to lose yourself and your voice amidst all of the noise and hustle bustle. To find peace and comfort in this ever-changing world, some people turn to religion, to Jesus or to Buddha. Others turn to doctors, psychiatrists and self-medication. I, on the other hand, turn to Cape Cod.

When I want to feel connected to a higher being, I don't go to church. I go surfing, fishing, shopping or sailing. I go for a walk on the beach and look up at the stars. In my opinion, Cape Cod has the ability to restore the youthful wonder we sometimes lose as we grow up. You're never too old to play like a kid and rediscover your inner child. It's always there, even if you can't see it. You just have to find it.

When the world gets to be too much, the Cape is my escape. When I feel crazy, tired and want to give up, the Cape restores my sanity and gives me the energy to keep on going. The sea, wind and waves have the ability to speak if you are willing to listen. They will teach you if you are willing to learn. When life gets me down, I don't need a shrink. I need Cape Cod Therapy.

ABOUT THE AUTHOR

Tom Simek was born and raised in upstate New York. He holds a Bachelors and Masters Degree in music composition, plays in a jazz band and resides with his wife Lara in Athens, Greece, where he teaches music and English as a second language. His other literary works in print include, "How to be Greek without Being Greek: A guide to Greece and living life" and the environmental children's book series "Eco-Fables: Green Stories for Children and Adults."

31967778R00071

Made in the USA
Charleston, SC
03 August 2014